being brothers and sisters

stories of personal need in the church

*Edited by
Diana Brandt*

Faith and Life Press
Newton, Kansas

Library of Congress Catalog Card Number 83-83062
International Standard Book Number 0-87303-091-5
Printed in the United States of America
Copyright © 1984 by Faith and Life Press
718 Main Street, Newton, Kansas 67114
This publication may not be reproduced, stored in a retrieval system, or transmitted in whole or in part, in any form or by any means, electronic, mechanical, photocopying, recording, or otherwise without the prior written permission of Faith and Life Press.

Illustrations by Les Brandt
Design by Jim Friesen

Printing by Mennonite Press, Inc.

*dedicated to my mother
who showed me that need
can bring forth
new possibilities*

PREFACE

It is much easier to define problems and give advice than to describe the reality of personal experience. The stories in this book have been told with courage and in the faith that understanding is the first step toward real change in a less than perfect world. In response, the primary question is not who is right or wrong, but how we can be honest with ourselves and sensitive with each other as we learn to become truly brothers and sisters.

A collection such as this cannot promise to be comprehensive or even typical; rather, it is hoped that the individual stories represented here will encourage others to express their needs and choose empathy rather than judgment in their responses to family members around them, whoever they may be.

You may want to use this book to generate discussion in various contexts such as adult Sunday school groups, K-groups, women's support groups, or study groups of various kinds. For this purpose we have included questions for reflection and discussion to help you get started (see pp. 111-115). While each story may be read separately, the study guide has been planned progressively, with each unit building on preceding ones.

It is important to respond personally and experientially as the writers in this collection have tried to do. This kind of discussion is not easy; it requires honesty, courage, and imaginative vision. But it may help us to understand each other so that together we may create new possibilities in relationship.

This book would not have come about without the encouragement and support of friends and family. Special thanks to Kathy Bergen for helping me think through the project, to David Schroeder for believing in it, and to my husband Les Brandt and daughters Lisa and Alison for living with it so many months. Thanks also to Heidi Harms for proofreading and a sympathetic ear.

                                                    Diana Brandt

INTRODUCTION

by David Schroeder

From our living room sofa we watched the first human being step on the moon. In his hand my father-in-law, Hugo Bartel, held a picture of the team of oxen he used to break the prairie sod on his homestead in Drake, Saskatchewan. He could not help but marvel at the changes he has witnessed in the span of his life.

In my much shorter life span, too, many changes have taken place. We now take technological progress for granted and expect it to continue at increasing rates. I am more impressed with the way the structures governing the relating of people to each other have changed. I am worried about what these changes will mean for humanity as a whole and for the Chrisitian community in particular.

After reading the stories in this collection, I found that almost every incident touched my own experience in some way. I was forced to reflect on my own life and growth from a new perspective. I found false impressions that needed correction, while other impressions were confirmed and strengthened. This open sharing has allowed me to re-evaluate my own experience.

I grew up in the Sommerfelder Mennonite Church. It was a community in which values—religious and other values— were instilled by authority and precedent rather than taught. We don't give children lengthy reasons for saying "he did that" rather than "he done that" ; we simply correct wrong usage by giving the correct usage. In my case religious and moral values were received in the same way. These values were taken for granted as part of the realities of this world.

This kind of spiritual and moral formation is powerful in its effects. It determines your life, your way of seeing, evaluating, and responding to experience. It cannot be easily challenged. It becomes part of your world view. But what do you do when you begin to realize, over time and many life experiences, that not all the values so communicated check with reality and perhaps not even with Scripture?

My family was a patriarchal family. My father made his decisions for the good of the family, but he made the decisions. Mother never really wanted to move to new places. She did not want to leave Sommerfeld and live in Blumenthal or Weidenfeld, Manitoba, nor Clearbrook, British Columbia, but she moved with her family to all these and more places because Father so decreed. Father decided when it was time to move, he handled the finances, and he determined the agenda for all ten of us in the family. Later I called into question this strong partriarchal pattern and rejected it.

When Father died, I realized how Mother had suffered under that system. She had kept her suffering to herself all the years of her marriage. But once she could trust herself to talk about it, she told how she tried to keep abreast of financial transactions that were never shared; how she sought to influence decisions without appearing to do so; how she suffered five spontaneous abortions besides giving birth to eleven children; and how she did not even tell father about all of them because he might be angry. I knew then that she had suffered much more than we ever realized. Actually they both suffered. They were caught in a structure under which neither was really free.

My rejection of the patriarchal pattern began early in life. The accepted male-female roles were a problem for me. After my older sister died, I was the youngest of seven boys (there were two younger sisters and a younger brother). As a result I had to do the "girls' work": make breakfast, wash dishes, clean the house, help with the laundry and milk the cows. I really didn't mind the work itself, but only that it wasn't "men's work"! By temperament I was also far from "macho" though I did excel in sports. I liked to cry over a good story, enjoyed needlework and was fond of drawing. Sometimes I thought my life would have been easier if I had been a girl.

But when I married I tried to take my patriarchal responsibilities seriously. I had to set the tone. Since I was also pastor of a church at this time, I left the children and the household work entirely to my wife. After all, I was doing the important work! Polio changed all that. My wife, Mildred, now took care of everything—the children, the household, myself, and all relations with others. From now on, when a nail was called for, I would hand the hammer to her because I could not manage it myself. She has been "the man around the house" these many years! But she has done it with more of a human touch.

In Germany where we lived for 2½ years we saw a patriarchalism that was even more extreme than the one I had known in my family, and we could begin to distance ourselves from it. The real opportunity for change, however, came after the death of Mildred's mother, when my father-in-law came to live with us. We became an extended family. Father-in-law was not patriarchal. His wife had shared in all decision making and was a leader in her own right in the family and in the community. We adopted more and more their family pattern. This has been a freeing thing for us in our marriage.

I grew up during the depression of the '30s. The farmers in the Altona area realized that in banding together they had better chances of survival. Cooperatives and Credit were organized. Various forms of mutual aid and self-help programs were begun. This thinking had a profound effect on me. It gave me a basic direction away from individualistic pursuits to more community and group-oriented programs and emphases.

The twenty years ('59-'79) of living as a three-generation family, inspired us to invite our daughter and son-in-law and their two children to live with us. They built an addition onto our house and so for two years (until my father-in-law's death) we had a four-generation household. Now we are three generations living together again. This means a different lifestyle for each of us, but it is a lifestyle that we cherish. I appreciate greatly the opportunity to relate daily to children and grandchildren.

The extended family is our way of saying that we need to do something to overcome the negative effects of the nuclear family, and to multiply the resources of the family. But we know that this is not possible for everyone to do, not even for all of our own children. Thus it should be seen more as a sign that we all need to be concerned about the patterns or structures of family life that are often determinative in shaping our lives. It should be a sign that we can influence some of the structures that shape or influence us.

We have, I believe, to a large extent moved away from the patriarchal family pattern, and have exended our family. These are things we could do—things over which we had some control. But there are many things in our lives over which we have no control, or very little control. In the past I found myself meeting people and situations from the standpoint that most things could be changed if we (they) would really act responsibly. Thus divorce, suicide, pollution of the environment, singleness, homosexuality etc. were seen as faults of persons rather directly. This is no longer satisfactory to me. It does not take into account the complexity of human freedom and social and material determinisms operating in our lives and in society. Nor does it take into consideration that others are free to act differently than we think they should or wish that they would.

I have come to appreciate much more our inability to achieve what we would like and see in how many ways life takes a turn that is not under our control and for which we cannot be directly praised or blamed. As a consequence I have come to see more clearly how we are caught in structures, movements, events, and responses that shape our lives but for which we are not directly responsible and for which we also cannot blame others. It has resulted in blaming persons less and being more concerned for people who are caught in events and realities not of their own choosing. Rather than blaming people, I ask myself how my own lifestyle is involved with others and in what way my choices act as determining factors in others' lives whether for good or evil.

We live in a network of interpersonal relationships. Our actions and attitudes touch the lives of others in ways that are not fully open to us. This is the more the case if we have not heard or understood each other or where we act in a prejudicial manner. If then we acknowledge that traditional ways of responding and acting are often prejudicial, we know that we can do untold damage to others by merely doing and saying what is acceptable in our culture.

Our first responsibility to each other as brothers and sisters in the Christian family, however, is to hear each other—to hear each other at the core or center of our lives. This involves putting ourselves in the other person's shoes; hearing from the other person's view or perspective. It involves listening to a person as a person who speaks out of a very specific set of experiences, settings, and events.

In this volume we have people sharing their experience with us openly and freely. These experiences are offered in the hope that we as brothers and sisters will learn to hear each other more fully, in a hope that we will hear voices we have not heard as clearly before, in the hope that we will learn to understand each other better and respond to each other more appropriately. We have a responsibility to exhort and admonish each other in the Lord but only after we have heard with a heart of love and concern those who share with us their experiences and convictions.

The various reports of personal experiences in this volume should cause us to ask what does this and that experience have to say to me. We need to make judgments, but that is different from being judgmental or prejudicial (i.e. to pre-judge). We need to be concerned for persons, all persons and therefore we need to hear each other and take each other's experiences seriously. May this volume help us to enter into other people's experiences and lives in a more helpful way.

TAblE of CONTENTS

Preface v
Introduction David Schroeder vii
1. Living in the Nuclear
    Family Abe and Elaine Bergen 1
2. Being Single Mary Mae Schwartzendruber 7
3. Being a Woman in a Man's World Anne Ens 16
4. Working Mother Mary Lou Driedger 24
5. Learning to Live with
    Disabilities Carol Friesen 35
6. Searching for Shalom in Mennonite
    Athletics Del Glick 44
7. Understanding Sexuality Keith C. Schrag 51
8. Parenting Parents Rose Barg 62
9. Life After Divorce Phyllis Vialoux 70
10. Losing a Mate Elfrieda Tiessen 75
11. Surviving Suicide Gayle Wiebe 86
12. Homosexuality: Two
    Perspectives Bev Scott, Kris Lane 92
13. Becoming God's People Lynne Martin 102
Questions for Reflection and Discussion 111

Chapter 1
Living in the Nuclear Family

by Abe and Elaine Bergen

Nine long months of planning and waiting were finally over. We were a "real" family at last. For several years we had been involved in discussions and experiments of community and communal living. There had not been any children; our focus had always been on the sharing of physical resources. We had come to believe strongly in mutual support, sharing of goods, and a broad definition of the family. But when our baby was born, we suddenly realized that a lot of our talk had been just that; in this crucial new venture we were on our own.

Far from an alternative family situation, we found ourselves cast in the typical roles of the typical nuclear family. Abe was employed full time; Elaine (having resigned from her job when the baby arrived) was to be a full-time mother. Both of us found this a frustrating situation: Abe felt "tied down" by his responsibilities as breadwinner and family supporter; Elaine felt depressed and lonely in her sudden isolation from society. Motherhood was not the wonderful event described in childbirth books; this realization came with a lot of attendant guilt.

What we had anticipated as an illuminating and unifying event became instead a terrible crisis. Where could we turn for help? Who could support us in our sudden nightmarish isolation? We were, after all, doing the typical, the "right" things. We were now a "real" family. But could this be what family life and parenting was really about?

A few months after Jeremy was born, we moved to Elkhart, Indiana, where Abe was enrolled in graduate studies at the Mennonite seminary. The move accentuated our loneliness. Away from family and friends, our needs intensified. Above the effort of coping with the tensions inside our little nuclear family, we needed to find the energy to make new friends, reach out for new supports. The nuclear family wasn't fulfilling its promise of "normal" happy living.

After a year at seminary, we decided to try a different parenting/working arrangement. Both of us would look for half-time employment outside the home, and we would share equally the responsibilities of homemaking and parenting. This seemed like an obvious solution to the needs we both felt. It was important for us to share our lives more completely, and at the same time to pursue our own individual callings. Friends assured us it wouldn't work. And it wasn't easy.

First of all, good half-time jobs are scarce. Employment caters to full-time workers; most part-time work is nonprofessional, poorly paid (and most of it is assigned to women). Secondly, we found ourselves in conflict with our own role expectations. Abe found part-time work threatening to his identity: "Half a job made me feel like half a person." As the only father on the playground Monday mornings, he experienced loneliness and a sense of failure, nonproductiveness. At work, comments like, "It must be nice to stay home half the week" reinforced this feeling. Elaine was left with a mountain of guilt for "depriving" her husband of his rightful career development by leaving "her" children in "his" care. Both of us overcompensated by doing more than our jobs required.

Our new family arrangement with its "buck-the-system" element was certainly more satisfying than the traditional roles we had escaped. But it added even more stress to our marriage. It became necessary to make joint decisions in every area of our life together. Who would do the laundry? the dusting? service the car? rake the leaves? Endless amounts of energy went into the arrangements of details that had previously been understood. The division of labor,

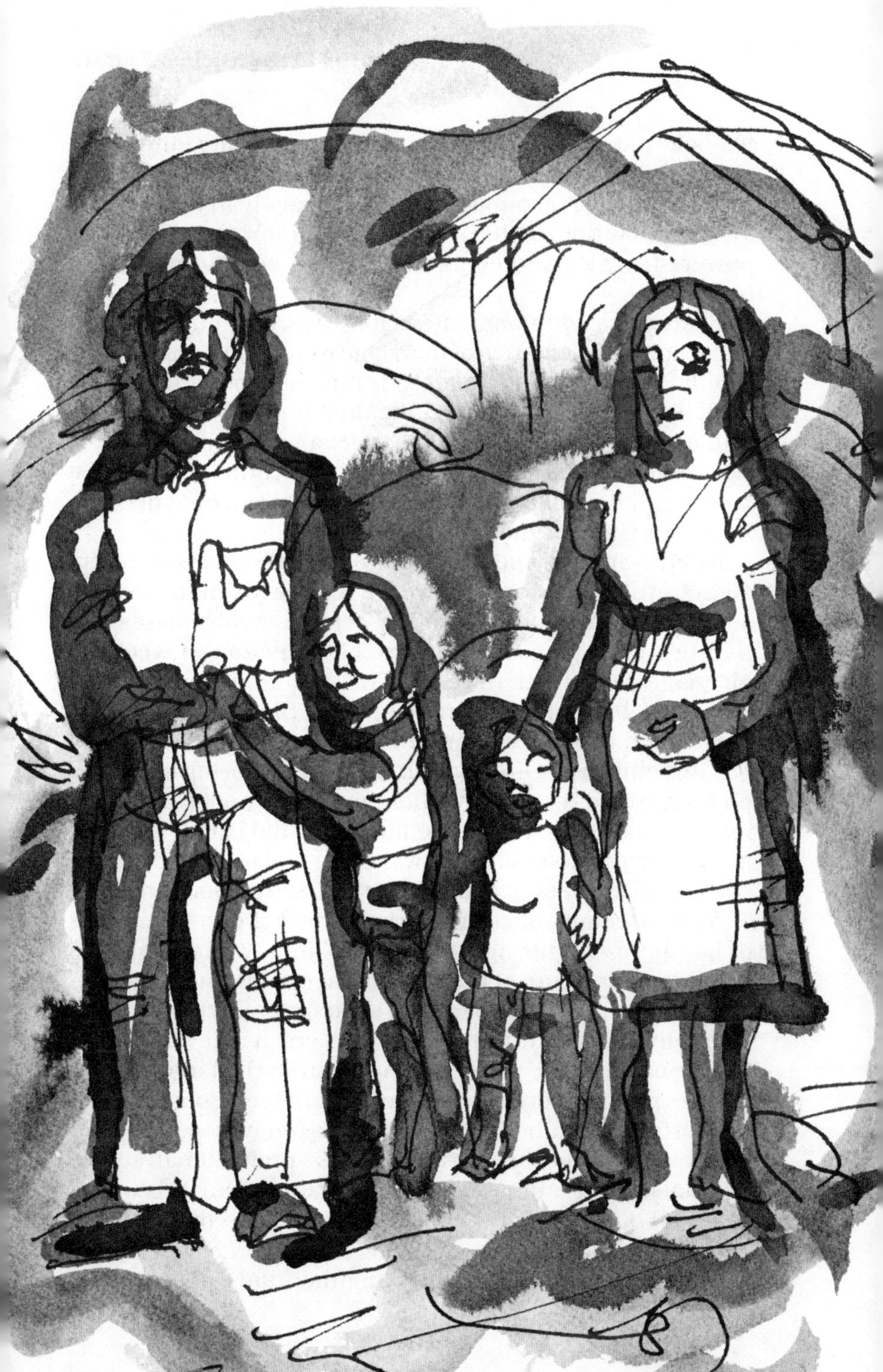

we believed, could be based on interest, ability, and available time rather than sexual stereotypes. But without role models, such an arrangement proved costly in time, effort, and expectation. Often we found ourselves engaged in power struggles and conflicts that had been unnecessary before.

There were additional internal pressures: Could we meet the emotional demands of marriage required by the nuclear family? Could we adequately fulfill each other's needs—socially, intellectually, romantically? It seemed unrealistic and ultimately destructive to expect a husband and wife to be everything and give everything to each other. There must be enough flexibility to allow some of our personal needs to be met outside the marriage relationship.

We encountered another dilemma. As a family with extensive church commitments, we felt torn between the responsibilities of parenting and other service involvements. We had begun to participate in the coordination of weekend Marriage Encounter retreats. This required frequent and extensive baby-sitting arrangements. Should faithfulness to God and the church community occur at the expense of our two children? Often we felt we were imposing ourselves on friends and relatives, without adequate opportunities to repay these debts. Equal exchange of child care with other families, a possible solution, was not a realistic option for us because of the busy schedule we had arranged for ourselves.

We were caught once again, this time in the crosscurrents of family restructuring. On the one hand, we had rejected the closed structure of the traditional family with its predetermined role patterns based on sexual stereotypes, in favor of greater flexibility and freedom in personal development. On the other hand, we felt alienated from the larger family with its rich network of intergenerational relationships and supports, and found ourselves increasingly dependent on impersonal child-care arrangements, professional advice manuals, and a confusing array of personal demands which canceled out much of the freedom we had so painfully acquired.

The nuclear family is clearly an inheritance of the industrial system with its hierarchical definitions intended to serve a male power base. Full-time work, as defined by business and industry, takes for granted an (unpaid female) supporting partner in the home. The women's movement has challenged this assumption and created new opportunities for recognition and validation for both men and women. But this has been achieved at great cost, and to some extent at the expense of children, who are increasingly left outside the complex arena of modern life. Is it possible to create alternative family patterns in an economic system which adheres to many of the rules of a discriminatory if not obsolete past?

The Hollywood version of love and romance does not adequately describe the needs of a marriage relationship. The "Waltons" kind of family with a parent or grandparent always there to provide traditional wisdom and patient assistance no longer exists for most of us. What kind of family patterns can we create to nurture and sustain each member of the family equally? What roles can we develop to give our children more freedom to develop according to their individual needs, without being cut off from their past and from the people around them? How can we begin to support each other again in the tasks of growing up, providing food and shelter, growing old, without sacrificing self-fulfillment and personal identity?.

Harried by jigsaw schedules and feeling a little "different," we have no regrets. Some people have told us they would like to try a family arrangement similar to ours, but that job demands or salary losses would be too great; or perhaps the risk of trying something different is too threatening. With our youngest child nearing school age, this particular arrangement may need reassessing and readjusting. The rewards have been tremendous: the flexibility to try new options and make real choices that were right and fulfilling for both of us has made family life not only bearable but truly exciting.

For us the birth of a child represented a major crisis in the nuclear family. For others, illness or separation or unemployment may be the event which cracks the veneer of this flawed social unit. As more and more people experience the inadequacy of an isolated and alienating living arrangement, will the Christian community unite in creating new and vital alternatives?

Abe and Elaine Bergen live in Winnipeg, Manitoba. Abe works as director of Youth Ministries for the Conference of Mennonites of Manitoba; Elaine is completing a master's degree in counseling at the University of Manitoba.

Chapter 2
being single

by Mary Mae Schwartzendruber

I am a single woman.
Not by misfortune
Nor by chance
But by choice.
Lest I be too proud, let me add,
Perhaps not by my own choice
Alone,
but with the help of choices others have made before me.
Yet now I have chosen again.
To be single can mean to be one-directional,
    Which alone is neither good nor bad
    But risks abuse.
My main direction is to be what I have been created,
    to do what I am called to,
    to have what is needful for this end.
All else is second, not constant,
    Helpful as it contributes to the first,
    Confusing and scattering in its distraction.
The first is deepest within me.
I am a single woman.
I am blessed in receiving the care of others.
I am claimed by the love of others.
And I don't always know how to live with the claims:
    "You mean so much to me. Give me more.
    I want to be with you (more)."
What are my demands?
    "You mean so much to me. I want to be with you
      sometimes.
    I need you, sometimes. I can and do live *alone*."

Is it possible
To be a single woman?
Is it completely selfish?
Is it rigidity at its height?
God help me!

It was the summer when I was twenty-three and preparing for an overseas assignment that I first recognized my singleness, with surprise and initial fear. I would be twenty-six years old on my return from Zaire, and still single! Until then, whether to marry or to stay single had not occurred to me. I was living well. . . professionally secure, with abundant friendships, a large family nearby, mobile in my nice big car, and not interested in serious dating. There was still so much I wanted to do. Teaching overseas was the newest, biggest adventure on the horizon. And it meant that I would be single when I was twenty-six years old. O.K. . . . on with life. Zaire, here I come.

Ten years, several continents, various jobs, and a lifetime of both healing and wounding experiences later, as I reflect on what it has meant for me to remain single, I recognize many issues that profoundly affect all adults, married or unmarried. Some concerns apply more specifically to those who are presently not living with a spouse. However, two-thirds of the Webster dictionary's definition of "single" does fit most people: a) alone, solitary, b) unmarried, c) consisting of one part, element, or member. According to this definition, birth and death are probably our most single moments. Our individuality always makes us single persons even if we are not all unmarried.

I was born single, and I have chosen not to alter that state. I could be single because I am widowed or divorced; a homosexual orientation might be reason to stay single; having a spouse that travels all the time would almost be "singleness"; I could be either wanting or waiting to get married or be delaying marriage for another five years until. . . ; or I could have taken a vow of celibacy for reasons of vocation. If you're guessing, it's "None of the above." No one has recently asked me, "Why aren't you married?" but I will venture to answer this common question, which is based on the assumption that marriage is the norm. I have not yet found enough reason to marry. Since my birth, I have experienced a variety of forms of community, and considered others, among them, marriage. I have cherished a variety of friends—male, female, Christian, atheist, old, young, some marriageable and many not, but I know of none with whom I would choose a permanent marriage bond. My meaning in life is to become what I have been created — a daughter of God — in the fullest way I know. Until now, while many relationships have significantly deepened this meaning, marriage has not seemed to be essential to it.

There have been many steps and detours along the way. One of the first was to establish who I was in relationship to my family, particularly my mother. The family pattern of spending many weekends in our parental home was an expectation to which I as an adult daughter no longer conformed. The memory of sitting at my dorm desk, thoughtfully penning a letter to my mother, is still clear. While I would always be her daughter, I no longer was her child, and I would treasure her friendship.

Establishig a new home through marriage is often the main means of separation from one's parental home. In our family, there has been tension between some of us over how much responsibility each is to assume in relation to our parents. At times, I wonder whether I have leaned so far toward separation that I'm less responsible as a family member than I could be. In any case, comparison with my siblings is not very helpful, since the circumstances of each one vary. However, single sons or daughters have often wrongfully borne the brunt of family expectations in regard to helping their parents, often actually living with them.

Today, one of my sisters and I have a home of our own. We are pleased to know a new mutuality in family hospitality. It is good to have a brother drop in unexpectedly and feel at home. My father rang the door bell and awakened us one summer morning, stopping in for breakfast on his way home from the airport. "Family is where you can come home at two in the morning and be welcomed" is a definition I have pondered.

"Who is my family?" a single person may ask. When I have lived far away from my biological family, I have struggled to determine the answer to that question. For example, in Zaire, my cry was, "I have no one to put me first!" Everyone else's spouse, children, home correspndence, and dog got a hearing before I did. To whom could I turn when I needed a place to belong? Twice I had been placed in a house with another single woman; twice there was a serious lack of communication. A family handily had me "house sit" for them while they were away on vacation — but their home wasn't readily available to me at other times.

In my last year, however, another single woman and I did choose to live together and to care for each other in various ways: household tasks, walks, talks, and leisure were shared. We assumed a certain "firstness" for each other. Each of us also found listening ears and warm relaxation in the home of an older missionary couple who had just moved nearby.

Later, in recalling the pain and the loneliness of many Zaire days, I spoke with a Protestant sister, herself celibate, about the difficulty of not being "first" to anyone. Couldn't Christian friends put each other first even outside of marriage? Did Jesus not value friendship above many other qualities? "Greater love has no one than this. . ." I mused.

Sister Albertine responded, "That's the whole point of being single. No one is first to you."

At the time I wrestled with the concept. That's right; I would agree that no one is more or less exclusively first, as in marriage. But surely in Christian community there are times when even a single person could be considered "first"! Rather than searching for a relationship that was exclusive, I wanted to be with people who were inclusive.

I am blessed with very significant primary relationships — my family, as well as male and female friends. I have chosen to live at the geographic hub of this circle of friendships. While families or married couples form a mini-community of their own, in our highly mobile society, a

Being Single

single person must choose with great care where to settle for a job. In determining in which locality to begin my ministry, I didn't reflect long. Ontario, where my family and long-time friends lived, was the only choice I considered. After years of moving, I needed roots: a home, a sense of belonging, and some semblance of "firstness," if I hoped to minister to anyone other than myself!

Few people are completely unattached to a biological family. However, when family ties are either nonexistent or weak, those who have not chosen the primary relationship of marriage create a "family" of their own. As a student in the United States, I was adopted by a couple as their sister, thus becoming an aunt to their children. This compensated for the affectionate, loving nieces and nephews I missed. In every place I have lived, close women friends have become sisters to me. Who but Kathy could I have telephoned at two o'clock that morning. A dear friend's mother was my Grandmammy, faithfully writing letters overseas. My home congregation formed a spiritual family, giving tangible evidence of their care. The intensity of these friendships changes with time and geography. These ties are less constant than immediate family ties, but the commitment to caring is renewed in each contact.

Commitment... the word strikes a new chord. For me, *commitment* and *adult* are closely related terms. How do I, a single person, know when I'm grown up? A friend recently confided in me that she and her husband were hoping to start a family any time now, and that she was pleased, because being a mother would show that she was adult even more than being a wife did. I listened, trying to understand her perspective, yet fearing the words. What lets me know I'm an adult, since neither wife nor mother are my roles?

I once heard my youngest brother say "She's not a woman, she's a lady. You're not a woman until you're married." Twenty years and "Women's Liberation" later — and the attitude is still evident!

I'm a woman. I'm an adult. I am committed to caring for others in responsible ways, and I receive care and love from others. That's grown up.

A widowed friend had difficulty reestablishing herself socially when her husband died. She just didn't feel comfortable anymore with her never-married friends whom she had known so well during her long years of singleness. "I just don't know what it is," she mourned. "It is as though I've lost status and am having to go backwards."

Her comment led me to reflect further on the status that marriage seems to give. Knowing that one is loved certainly brings self-acceptance more easily, but learning love and self-acceptance is a task for everyone, married or single. Faithfulness is a gift—not only for a marriage relationship, but also among peers, with friends, or as a church member. Learning to enjoy and luxuriate in solitude is a Christian grace that is perhaps more essential and more strenuous in marriage than in singleness. Wholeness and brokenness are part of each human story whether or not the story is set in the context of marriage.

Singleness is sometimes perceived in a degrading way. Just a few days ago, I heard a married man contradict himself as he discussed dating with a group of students. First, he said that dating a variety of people was helpful and healthy. Then, he jokingly told them not to wait too long to settle down, or all the nice ones would be taken. To my dismay, the "leftover" syndrome is still hanging around. I feel like a whole, committed, rather "nice" adult, and I long for the day when single people won't need to struggle against discriminatory stereotypes.

At the root of the struggle to be both single and whole, some cultural and theological values become interwoven in a complex way. Culturally, the romantic ideal—one person to fulfill all of our needs in an intense, meaningful relationship—has a stranglehold on us. Its ramifications are vast. First, it is assumed that there is a Mr. or Ms. Right for everyone, and that those who can't find that one aren't normal. Some persons change from partner to partner, either in search of the "one," or cynically proving that it's all nonsense. Others never find the "one," and so stay alone. Many experience the disappointment and grief of losing the romantic glitter in marriage, and can't cope with what is left

Being Single

of the relationship. Not only disappointing singleness but also disappointing marriage lead to a serious critique of this value.

An opposing tendency is to propose that no one person should meet too many of another single person's needs in too intense a way. Margaret Evening in *Who Walks Alone* warns of the dangers of close friendship between women, for example. The questions of jealousy, becoming too rooted through the relationship, and becoming exclusive are not questions of singleness alone; marriage also carries those risks.

The theological value of sexuality gets confused by the cultural romantic ideas. Sexuality, as I understand it, is the gift and the obligation of being created male or female individually, as well as male and female in community.[1] The latter has often been understood primarily as coital relationship, thus making marriage the highest good. The romantic ideal reinforces this interpretation, and singleness becomes abnormal. But what has happened, I ask, to the fellowship of male and female outside of the marriage bond? If sexuality were seen as the expression of both my female-ness and my fellowship with others (female and male), the present undue emphasis on genital relationship would diminish. Further, the church could state unequivocally with Nancy Hardesty that God created every human being for relationship and love, not necessarily for marriage.[2]

The United Church of Canada's statement on sexuality, *In God's Image. . . Male and Female*, states that "When sexuality is broadly understood, there is an enormous range of sexual expression apart from intercourse available to all of us. . . " (p. 68). It is a fact, however, that sexual intercourse is not restricted to marriage in today's culture. The church's stance on monogamous marriage with its "Wait" and "Don't" imperatives to young people and single adults does not conform to this social reality. In a society that is booming with sex manuals, erotic movies, music crammed with sexual images, and the license of a so-called "sexual revolution," the church seems to have chosen the path of repeating the traditional mores and, in silence, ignoring the realities.

Those adults, single and married, who are not living by the church's mores, find sources of dialogue and healing outside of the institution which labels certain sins of sexual expression as the worst.

How can the church respond more helpfully? Let the church begin to speak to and demonstrate unapologetically the enjoyment of touch, affection, closeness, and warmth as forms of sexual expression for all. I am grateful that Christian literature on masturbation is becoming less judgmental, more realistic and humane than in the past.[3] I would encourage the church to engage its single people in discerning dialogue to allow them to become more aware of and intentional in their sexual expression. Small group dialogue would prevent both a mindless following of society's sexual license and a thoughtless acceptance of traditional norms which might prove inadequate under critical testing. I joyfully bear witness to the fact that some Christian friends have listened to me, discussed with me, questioned me, and forgiven me in my journey toward grateful acceptance of my sexuality.

I am a single woman. I feel loved and beautiful most of the time, enjoying other people and feeling comfortable with them. I am blissfully unaware of married people who feel awkward in my company. At a recent wedding, I joined the groom's family table. Though we were scarcely acquainted, we enjoyed a hearty conversation. Halfway through the meal, we noticed that one glass was missing, presumably because a ninth place setting had been added. Nine people. . . I was the only uncoupled one, I finally realized! An error had drawn to my attention the previously unnoticed fact. Once again I learned that both in my own eyes, and probably in the eyes of others, I am how I see myself.

I am a single woman. At times, I feel lonely, frightened, and insecure. At other times, my aloneness is rich, freeing, and still. Frequently I realize that my singleness is a gift that reminds me of the truth expressed so well by Bruce Yoder in *Single Voices*:

>To be whole is to be in community;
>to be whole is to stand alone. . .

We are alone; we are together.
We are complete; we are imcomplete.[4]
In the ways I live, I wish to celebrate aloneness and togetherness, freedom and commitment, biological and spiritual family, maleness and femaleness. I want to be open to marriage as well as singleness, respecting the contribution of each to the growth of the kingdom of God on earth.

It is possible to be single and whole.

Mary Mae Schwartzendruber is co-pastor of the Stirling Avenue Mennonite Church, Kitchener, Ontario.

Notes
1. Paul K. Jewett, *Man As Male and Female* (Grand Rapids: Erdmans, 1975), was very helpful in clarifying this concept.
2. In *Solo Flight*, ed. Jim Towns, (Wheaton, Ill.: Tyndale House, 1980), p. 26.
3. J. B. Nelson, *Embodiment* (Augsburg, 1978), pp. 168-73, is a good example of this. I do question, however, the organization of this chapter on "The Morality of Sexual Variations," since he begins the chapter with "Sex and the Unmarried"—seemingly the first variation!
4. (Scottdale: Herald Press, 1982), pp. 86, 92, in the excellent chapter "Singleness and Spirituality: Holy Loneliness."

Chapter 3
bEiNq A WOMAN iN A MAN'S WORLd

by Anne Ens as told to Diana Brandt

I work as a tax auditor for the federal government of Canada. This is a job traditionally assigned to men. The ratio of men to women in my office, the audit section of Taxation in Winnipeg, is ten to one. Five years ago, when I started, there were five women tax auditors out of 150. The tax audit department is organized hierarchically: higher management is chosen from lower management, strictly according to rank. There is only one woman in a supervisory position in tax audit in Winnipeg. Women generally don't seem to get selected for initial supervisory positions which are the prerequisite to further promotion. No woman has been asked to sit on a selection board for a supervisory position in tax audit in the history of this office.

Is equal opportunity for women attainable in the "white male system"?[1] There are basically two ways of fighting discrimination in the office. One is by personally defending women's rights whenever they are denied or abused. This is a lonely and costly endeavor. One must be willing to risk friendships and lose contacts. This is so even if one is part of an organized support group such as Equal Opportunities for Women.[2] The other is to work quietly for promotion and then use one's power to make changes. This is a lengthy process which involves a lot of compromise. By the time a woman reaches a position of influence, she has become as much a part of the hierarchy that it is almost impossible to take a stand on basic issues. In my experience, both ways have been difficult, hazardous, and lonely.

When I began working in this office, I openly resisted discrimination as I experienced it. I pointed out inconsistencies in expectation and attitude to co-workers and supervisors. I refused to listen to pornographic jokes. I corrected sexist language used by men around me, e.g. "broad," "girl." This behavior earned me the reputation of being "abrasive" and a "communist bitch." People would say to me, "Anne, why don't you play it cool for a while, until everybody likes you, and *then* do something?"

Two years ago, one of the men in my office put up a poster near his desk depicting a partially nude woman in a sexually suggestive pose advertising "Suzy Cream Cheeze" shorts. I, along with another woman friend, pointed out the inappropriateness and discriminatory nature of this poster to the supervisor and asked (politely) to have it removed. He did so immediately; no confrontation was necessary. Within minutes the entire office knew that Anne had "ripped Jim's poster off the wall." The response was vicious. I was socially ostracized for a month.

The issue remained contentious for at least half a year (and is still referred to on occasion). My support group during this time was a very small group of women friends. I was told I had ruined my career chances. The women in the office found themselves with conflicting loyalties. To the men they denied that the poster had offended them; to me privately some said, "I pretended it wasn't there." After a day of silent hostility I would sometimes find a note on my car, "Yes, I am really your friend, Anne." At this time I began to feel as if I was working against myself: instead of defending women's rights, I was making our life more difficult.

The fact that such a small incident could trigger so much hostility is surprising but not incomprehensible. It was, after all, a political act. "Decent" religious family men in the office found themselves defending a photograph they would not have allowed into their homes. They had never thought of themselves as "dirty guys." "It was the *way* you did it, Anne," they said. What they could not see was that there was no other way to get it done without causing even greater offense.

Many of these people have since become my friends. I am no longer personally threatening to them. My values have not changed, but what was perceived as an isolated aggressive act can now be seen for what it was, an expression of a consistent attitude of respect for women's dignity. The price I paid for this understanding was "sticking it through" for two very difficult years. Women who have experienced similar opposition often quit long before this (and few private situations offer comparable job security).

Everyone has a breaking point: mine I think would have been to experience physical advances in this period of psychological rejection. Because I had violated a role expectation, I was subjected to all the techniques of office warfare—hostility, professional criticism, and sexual come-ons. Touching, for me, would have been the ultimate manipulation; a physical appeal for my affection which was intended as a put-down would have put me in an intolerable position.

Recently, my involvement in office politics has taken a different turn. Six months ago I became eligible for a term position as training officer in my department. My supervisor pressured me to drop my involvement with Equal Opportunities for Women as a condition for the promotion. The reason he gave was that it takes too much time. This was not a legitimate request since the coordination of EOW activities in Taxation is a director-appointed position created by the Treasury Board.

I had to make a decision: either lodge a formal complaint with the director, thereby alienating my supervisor for the duration of our term together, or comply with the request and give up my activities with EOW. We reached an agreement: time spent on EOW activities would be mutually arranged. As a result, I have spent very little time coordinating EOW activities in the office as a training officer; arranging the time became asking a favor. This is called "being nice"— it is less painful than fighting open hostility, but I am left feeling compromised and dissatisfied: "being nice" certainly doesn't get things done either. In this case a private transaction saved face for my supervisor and secured my promotion, but it guarantees nothing for my successor. That is why I have decided to lodge a formal complaint after my term has ended: not for revenge but to protect the next person in this situation from having to pay the same price. As a result, the coordination of EOW activities will be spelled out in a job description, and denial of rotation or advancement on the basis of EOW involvement will be forbidden. As Judith Finlayson points out in her article, "Power in the Public Sphere" (*Homemakers*, November, 1982), the history of women has been silent. There have not been role models for our individual successes. Women must advance themselves alone. But this can be changed.

A woman pays for defending her rights; she also pays for success. Because I have been "successful" in coordinating an effective EOW program in our office, there is a rumor that, "What Anne wants, Anne gets." Insinuation of this kind has the effect of denying the very hard work involved in winning rights for women. It is not simple to coordinate seminars on career planning, assertiveness training, sexual harassment, to plan consciousness-raising activities such as a dual career-families workshop; it is even more difficult to persuade the director that the need exists for such activities.

A woman's advancement, however small, will inevitably be greeted with, "Sure. You got legs." or "Well. We know how *you* got your promotion." Sexual innuendo is probably the most pervasive and damaging form of discrimination in the office world. Men have been conditioned to think of women as mothers and lovers and wives. It is very difficult for them to develop a working relationship with women as colleagues and supervisors and friends. There is a tendency to put women back into the familiar roles. This is often unconscious and even well-intended. Instead of telling a woman, "You did a good job," a man will respond to work well done with "You're pretty" or "You made the room smell nice when you walked in." After my first day teaching audit procedures, a colleague commended me with "You looked real sexy up there, Anne."

Efforts to teach men a different way of relating to women are usually met with extreme hostility; they were trying to be nice, after all. It is almost impossible for a man to recognize the way in which sexual banter (however flattering and well-meant) undermines and destroys a woman's status as a colleague. After viewing *Workplace Hustle*, a film depicting sexual harassment in the workplace, one of the men in my office responded, "But what would a woman think if she wasn't harassed at least once in her life," a comment which reveals not only insensitivity but willful ignorance about the meaning of harassment.[3]

Women have been victims of this kind of thinking for a long time, but it is only recently that we have begun to speak out against it. One of our most important weapons against sexual stereotyping and harassment is bonding with each other. Over the past year, the women in my office have developed a tradition of going for lunch together on Fridays. There has been a lot of opposition to this from men. "It's unprofessional," they say, and "The caliber of your work is going down." This criticism hits women at our most vulnerable point: the need to prove our competency in a "man's" field (over and over!). Since the men have been going for lengthy "liquid lunches" on payday for years, it is clear that the opposition stems from another direction. What is threatening is the idea that women can get their identity from each other: men are afraid of this, for if they are no longer needed to give (sexual) approval to women, they will have to begin relating to women as true colleagues and equals. Such a revolution could change office politics and indeed the entire social fabric so radically that it is breathtaking to imagine the possibilities. Envision a tax audit department that is not tied to the white male system and its rules: hierarchy, denial of subjective reality, systemic discrimination. Envision a society in which the work that women do and the talents that women have are of equal value to men's work and ability, in which "work" and "family" are not separate and contradictory categories, but mutally supportive and interrelated social units, in which intuition and personal autonomy support and qualify competence and success, in which sex is not a bid for power but a free meeting of equals.

Do women make good tax auditors? Experience has shown that where women excel in this high stress, sometimes called "belligerent" work, is in its interpersonal aspect. Women find it easier to establish confidential relationships with taxpayers; they have an intuitive sense of what approach is needed to get necessary information. They are less prone to the kind of high pressure tactics that create antagonism and mistrust in the public. Where women fall down is in processing the actual file to completion. It takes them longer, and their knowledge of how the system acutally works is less complete. This is understandable, since women have on the one hand had to develop intuitive skills to deal with those in power, and on the other, have been deprived of the "buddy system" by which men often gain their most valuable insights into the system. A woman may need to spend hours of laborious research to discover what her male colleague finds out painlessly in five minutes over coffee with a supervisor.

Evaluation generally concerns itself only with the latter skill since it is difficult to measure the ambiguity of human relations. If women can be given the same breaks and the same support in the system as men, they can learn to succeed on equal terms. If men can learn to recognize what have been traditionally women's strengths, the system can be changed to accommodate a much wider range of skills; "intuition" can also be developed by men.

Women who do succeed in the system are often caught off guard by the peer pressure to prove themselves, by the personal ambition that a hierarchical system engenders. Men have been conditioned to take this for granted. All of us need to become aware of the limitations a competitive hierarchy imposes on human development, and to help create new, more cooperative models in which people can learn to live and work and play together as equals.

The Mennonite church has not, by and large, supported the struggle for women's rights in the workplace. One reason for this is ignorance: my parents, for example, find my experiences in the office either exaggerated or in some way "asked for." Mennonites have chosen to ignore many of the built-in injustices of the system we have become part of. Another more pervasive reason is the status of women in the church itself. Because (female) submission to (male) authority is widely preached and accepted, defending women's rights often becomes a subversive act; it is perceived as a direct threat to home and family and traditional values. It is sometimes felt that women deserve the problems they encounter in their struggle for independence and equality.

Mennonite businesses and institutions may not tolerate the degree of sexual explicitness prevalent in a government office, but the power structure is the same. (It is just more insidious.) Women are expected to play a supportive role to male management; advancement for women is as difficult. Many Mennonites feel strongly that "a woman's place is in the home" and therefore refuse to support day-care and other affirmative measures; "home" and "work" are kept intentionally separate and therefore in conflict.

Because the Anabaptist rebellion was aimed at many of the same systemic inequities that women are fighting in our time, it is disheartening to see how little the Mennonite church is contributing to this struggle today. As a daughter in a tradition which holds in theory at least to the equality of all persons before God, I await the time when the vision of our foremothers and fathers reaches fulfillment.

Anne Ens works as a tax auditor for Taxation Canada in Winnipeg, Manitoba.

NOTES
1. I borrow this term from Anne Wilson Schaef in her revealing study of sexual politics, *Women's Reality*, (Winston Press, 1981).
2. Equal Opportunities for Women is a federally funded program which assists individuals and groups in the organization and implementation of affirmative action plans. EOW policy is "to ensure that within a reasonable period of time representation of male and female employees in the public service approximates the proportion of qualified and interested persons of both sexes available, by department, by occupational group and by level."
3. The Public Service Alliance of Canada defines sexual harassment as

"behavior related to sexuality that may be verbal, physical, deliberate, unsolicited or unwelcome. It is a real or implied threat to economic security and causes emotional stress." Research indicates that more than 70 percent of working women have experienced sexual harassment at some time.

Chapter 4
WORKING MOTHER

by Mary Lou Driedger

I am a woman with two full-time jobs. I am a teacher and a mother. I love both of my jobs. I am good at both of them. But it isn't always easy to manage two such demanding careers at the same time. During my four years of parenting/teaching there have been crisis times when I have had to deal with ambivalent feelings in myself and in the attitudes of my husband, my child, my friends and relatives, my colleagues and employers, my church and my community.

For as long as I can remember I always wanted to be a teacher. My favorite game as a child was playing school. I would be the teacher and my brothers and sisters and neighborhood friends the pupils. When I got married at age nineteen and my husband was unsure about what he wanted to do, I immediately applied to a one-year teacher certification program. I had enjoyed my two years at college, but I was anxious to get on with my career. I was happy to postpone further study and get to work. I liked teaching as much as I had thought I would, and I soon began to realize that I was very good at what I did. I liked the fact that my job made it possible for me to meet and work with so many different people. Teaching could be as interesting and rewarding as I wanted to make it. I got real satisfaction from working hard on new projects, programs, and materials. I felt good about the positive responses to my work from the children, their parents, my colleagues, and supervisors. I felt I had found my niche, my "calling."

I taught in Winnipeg for two years, after which my husband and I both accepted teaching jobs in the rural Mennonite community where I had grown up. I began taking night classes at the University of Manitoba and was excited about trying out new approaches and ideas in my classroom. I started an association for the kindergarten teachers in our school division. We worked hard on preparing materials for parents whose children were beginning school, and developing new curriculum ideas. I served on the executive of our local teachers' association and was given the job of setting up a teacher resource center for our school division.

The spring of 1978 was a significant one for me. One Friday morning my principal called me into his office to say that I was being offered the position of associate principal in my school. I was excited, but asked to think about it over the weekend. That same Friday after school, I went for a pregnancy test which was confirmed as positive. On Monday I explained the situation to my principal. Since I would be absent for more than half of the coming school year, it would be wiser to select someone else for the position.

I wanted the baby. It was a planned pregnancy. But I also wanted the promotion. Having to choose between them seemed unfair. If I had been a man I could have accepted the new position whether or not I was going to have a child. The timing was unfortunate. But in the excitement of becoming a mother, I consoled myself with the prospect of other offers in the future.

I have had to cope with these same mixed feelings over and over in the last four years. The first day I left Joel to go back to work was a very difficult one. I was anxious and eager to return to my job. I had found my maternity leave revitalizing; a time to enjoy my child and to think about and cultivate new ideas for teaching. Often at night, when I got up to feed Joel at 2 a.m. or 4 a.m., I made mental plans for my classroom for the fall. Nevertheless, I was crying hard as I drove away from the baby-sitter's house the first day I left him there.

Another crisis came when Joel was two years old. I was asked to consider the position of principal in an elementary school about fifteen miles from where we lived. Again I was eager to try the new challenge, and felt good about the position. Again I turned it down. The first year or two would require a great deal of after-hour office work. Although I was used to bringing home a full briefcase, much more of my work as a principal would have to be done at the school. Also, since the school was some distance away, the extra drive in the morning and after school would mean leaving Joel earlier in the morning and picking him up later. At the same time being a principal was considered a long-term commitment, since it took one or two years just to become familiar and comfortable with the position. Would my employers be happy if I left in two or three years to have another child? In light of all these considerations I felt I had to refuse the position. I still hope a similar offer will come in the future, but one wonders how often such offers will be made if continually refused. I am trying to understand and cope with my conflicting inner feelings of career advancement versus family life.

Another conflict for me personally has centered around whether I can be as good a mother if I am also a teacher, and whether I can be as good a teacher if I am also a mother.

In many ways I realize teaching has made me a better mother. My teaching gives me self-confidence, a feeling of worth, and happiness. This makes me a better person for my child to relate to. Because I am away from Joel so much of the day, I am more aware of spending quality time with him during our evening and holiday times together. My teaching career has been a source of many good experiences for Joel. He loves to come to my classroom with me and read, listen to records, color, play, or pretend while I am working. I invite all my students to our home during the year. After their initial visit, many return again on their own, or my family is invited to visit in their homes. In this way Joel has come to know many of my students as friends. It has been good for him to get to know these children, some of whom have homes and backgrounds quite different from his own.

Yet, there are days when I come home tired and irritable, after a particularly frustrating day at work, and I do not have the patience with Joel that I should. Sometimes I have had to miss programs and social events at the church or daycare that Joel was involved in, because they were in the afternoon while I was working. When Joel exhibits undesirable behavior or expresses ideas which I disapprove of, I wonder if he would have developed these same actions and opinions if I had been home with him. I find myself constantly weighing the pros and cons of teaching while mothering.

When I first began teaching after Joel was born, it was important for me to prove that I could be just as good a teacher with the added responsibility of motherhood. I almost felt a need to prove to my colleagues that Joel would not interfere with my ability to do my job well. Although it has meant adjusting my work schedule so I can take more of my work home, I have still managed to maintain a progressive program I am happy and satisfied with. In many ways motherhood has made me a better teacher. I have more patience and tolerance with the children because I have a child of my own. It is easier for me to understand parents' worries and frustrations. I think sometimes that knowing I am a parent has made my students' parents more comfortable and at ease talking with me. I certainly have a much greater appreciation for the role of the parent and all the responsibilities that entails.

My husband's feelings and attitude toward my job have been very important to me. Dave has never been opposed to my career. When I first began working a year after we were married, he left most of the household tasks to me. This was quite natural, since he had come from a home where his mother had always managed to put in a full day's work in the field and still cook, clean, and care for her husband and five sons. When our son was born, Dave enjoyed caring for him and spending time with him, but I was still in charge of Joel's physical needs and finding baby-sitters.

When I became pregnant Dave expressed no concern about my returning to work shortly after the baby's arrival. However, after Joel was born he began to worry. Would we find someone good enough to look after our son? Dave even talked of quitting work himself to stay home. He was having second thoughts. Finally he realized I just wasn't happy at home. He reasoned that if I wasn't happy how could he and Joel be happy? He accepted my enthusiastic reassurances that the woman I had found to look after Joel was warm and loving and capable.

Once I started teaching again Dave began slowly to realize that it was difficult for me to handle so much responsibility alone. We now share cooking, shopping, and some household duties. Dave was instrumental in planning for Joel's switch from a private home baby-sitter to a day-care; and we work together as chairpersons of the maintenance committee at Joel's day-care.

I feel that my going back to teaching has encouraged Dave to take more responsibility and time for our son. This is not to say I have managed to cope completely with my husband's attitudes toward my job. I still often feel I carry the bulk of the household and child-care responsibilities. I still get irritated by Dave's resentment of the extra time I spend on my school work at home. However, we both realize that my teaching has in many ways added vitality and interest to our life together. We are learning and growing together as we work at the conflicts that must arise in any marriage where both parents work outside the home.

I have been fortunate in having a happy, well-adjusted child who makes friends quickly and naturally, and adapts easily to new situations. My son's easygoing nature has made my working outside the home much less complicated and frustrating than it might have been. For two years he received loving and protective care in a private home. When he was ready for more freedom and companionship he let us know by expressing his dissatisfaction verbally and emotionally. He has been happy at his day-care since the first day. He calls it his "special school." He says, "My mom goes to school, my dad goes to school and I go to school." I realize that had Joel been a withdrawn or overly sensitive child it would have been much more difficult for him to adjust to being away from home all day. Although he may prove me wrong in the future, right now he seems to feel no resentment or negative feelings about my not being at home with him. As far as he is concerned our situation is natural and the way things have always been. His daily routine is familiar, consistent, and comfortable for him.

I am very close to my parents. Their opinions, feelings, and attitudes are important to me. My father has always believed in working hard. As children we were continually reminded to make something of ourselves. Dad encouraged us to be successful at whatever we chose to do and always expected nothing but our best. I know this has been an influence in my decision to continue with my teaching career. As a teacher I feel I am putting my talents to their best use. Although Dad has always been proud of my successes as a teacher, he was strangely quiet when my return to work after Joel's birth became a topic of discussion. When I was offered the principalship two years later, Dad's concern was that "I should be looking for ways to spend more, not less, time with Joel now that he was getting older."

My grandfather always impressed upon us children the importance of getting an education and putting it to good use. He was sad about his own lack of education, which had been interrupted by the Russian Revolution. He was never prouder of his grandchildren than when we graduated from high schools, colleges, and universities. However, when I decided to return to work after Joel was born, Grandpa had little to say about my college or university education being put to good use. To him it was inconceivable that I would choose to leave my baby and go back to work, and he told me so. Over the past four years his attitude has mellowed, but whenever we are together he still questions me, often in a joking and affectionate way, about whether I still like my job, about Joel's day-care arrangements and whether it isn't time for Joel to have a brother.

My mother's own experiences and support have perhaps been the most important factors in my returning to teaching after Joel was born. When I was small my father was attending medical school. He worked at odd jobs when he wasn't studying. That left my mother to bring up three small children and run a boarding house for university students in the upper two stories of our home. In order to bring in the money needed to care for our family and support my dad's schooling, she cleaned, cooked, and laundered for a houseful of students. A former teacher, and accomplished musician with a college education, she never for a minute thought of getting someone to look after us children and return to work as a teacher to bring in the necessary funds. It just wasn't done. But she told me later of her frustration. No one seemed worried about her fulfillment or feelings. In spite of her hectic work schedule she always seemed to find many moments in her busy days to spend quality time reading, singing, and playing with her children. This has been an encouragement to me as I try to find and spend quality time with my own child.

My mother has been supportive throughout my teaching/mothering career. She has always expressed her pride in me and my career and has been understanding of my need to work outside the home. She has always been ready to babysit when Joel has been sick or other child-care arrangements fell through. When I finally completed my B.A. a year after Joel was born and after six years of summer and night courses, she was the one who came to the graduation exercises. My husband thought I was silly even to go to the ceremony; the rest of the family was too busy; but Mom was taking pictures and smiling with tears in her eyes when I came down the steps with my diploma.

She is so eager to help me that it has become necessary for us to make an honest agreement. I will only call her to care for Joel if the need arises on the condition that she will always let me know if she had other plans, even vague ones. This way I can be reasonably sure that she is giving her own needs and plans priority.

My colleagues and friends have, on the whole, been supportive of my return to teaching. I have sometimes received comments such as, "If the Lord blesses you with a child, I don't see how you can desert that child," or "How can you let someone else bring up your child?" Sometimes when children come to school clothed inadequately for the weather or without breakfast, a colleague will remark, "Well, her mother works, you know," implying that she doesn't have time to look after her children properly. I try to take these remarks in stride and not become too defensive.

The attitude of my employers toward my return to work came as something of a surprise to me. My baby was due in February, so I planned to teach until Christmas and return to work the following September. According to my contract I was really only entitled to maternity leave till the middle of May. I was sure, though, that the superintendent would see fit to extend my maternity leave since it would be better for my students not to have their study year interrupted twice.

I was very surprised then to be called to the superintendent's office for a chat one afternoon. I sat down and he began, "I just want to say from the outset, Mary Lou, that I don't believe mothers of young children should work. Their place is in the home. I'm going to advise you the way I would if you were my own daughter. I've known you since you were a little girl and I care about your welfare. I'm sure this is the kind of thing your own father would say too." He then proceeded to advise me to resign from my position rather than extend my maternity leave. He was fairly certain I would change my mind about wanting to come back once I'd had the baby, but if I didn't he promised me I could have my former position back.

I guess my initial reaction was one of hurt. Both my husband and I had worked hard for this school division. I'd sat on all sorts of committees and boards, Dave had coached numerous sports teams and directed plays, and we'd chaperoned a class trip at our own expense and on our own time. I thought we'd gone "the second mile" as employees and now our employer was turning down a reasonable request for extension of maternity leave. It was a slap in the face.

My superintendent assured me that Dave and I were valuable employees, but by granting me extended maternity they would be setting a dangerous precedent. It might appear that they were encouraging women to take maternity leaves and condoning the practice of mothers of young children returning to work.

My hurt feelings turned to anger. I called the Manitoba Teachers Society and the lawyer there advised me that they could take my case to court. Since my contract said a teacher could request and receive extended maternity leave if the board and superintendent deemed her request reasonable, they felt I had legal ground to stand on. My teaching record was good and my request for leave more than reasonable.

I suggested this option to my principal and colleagues. Although they sympathized with me, they felt that in our small, predominantly Mennonite community I'd be making a big mistake. The court case would cause hard feelings, bring bad publicity, and possibly make working in the community uncomfortable for both my husband and me in the future. So I resigned. I gave up my tenure, job seniority, accumulated sick days, job security, health and life insurance, and went home to have my baby.

Over the last four years, my employer's stance toward working mothers has softened somewhat, perhaps mainly because so many women are choosing to return to teaching after their pregnancies. However, when I served on the teachers' negotiating team during contract talks last year, we were still unable to convince the board to allow anything more concrete concerning extension and granting of maternity leaves to be added to our contract.

When we enrolled Joel in our local day-care center at age 2½ and I offered to serve on the board of directors, I came face to face with my community's attitude toward working mothers. Serving on the board has been an educational, frustrating, and time-consuming experience. The day-care receives little support from the parents whose children attend it, from the businesses in the community, from the school division, or from the churches in the community. The first annual day-care parents' meeting I attended was an eye-opener for me. Sixty children attend my son's day-care at various times each week, either part-time or full days, but only 12 out of the 120 parents attended the meeting. The response is similar when we stage fund-raising projects or cleanup and workdays. Most parents use the day-care as a business. They pay their fees, leave their child, and pick him or her up. They ignore the many many volunteer hours and extra dollars needed to keep the day-care open. Government funding and parent fees enable us to pay for the daily upkeep of the day-care. But any extras, like toys, art supplies, playground equipment and books must be purchased with money from fund-raising projects.

In our town this is difficult. Since the prevailing attitude is still that mothers should be at home with their children, few people are willing to contribute funds. Even though the day-care provides a valuable service for the employees of many businesses in town, those same businesses will not donate money when asked. Parents are also not willing to give extra money to day-care. Many can afford to spend thirty dollars for a trip to the city and a ticket to a Winnipeg Jets game, but would not consider paying the same amount to someone to care for their child for the day. Although some parents receive government subsidies for day-care fees, most in our fairly affluent community can afford to give a considerable amount above the minimal daily fee.

There is a high turnover in staff. We can only afford to pay our workers minimum wage, so many leave for the chicken-killing plant or window factory where wages are higher. It is virtually impossible to get people with university or community college degrees in child-care because we can't afford to pay them the wages they deserve. The government, while providing some funding, limits the amount parents can be charged so we can't look to that source for increased revenue.

Since our community has no established nursery schools, many people enroll their children in day-care one or two mornings a week for nursery school experience. In the city, nursery school programs are often part of, and funded by, the school system. In our town almost one-third of the children who enter kindergarten in our elementary schools each fall have attended one of the town's two day-cares either part or full time. The day-cares are therefore providing an important educational experience for young children prior to their entering the school system. Yet we receive no financial support from the school division. And since the administration is presently looking for ways to cut costs, we cannot hope to find support there in the near future.

The many Mennonite churches in our town provide no support whatever to day-care. I find this puzzling and disheartening. I read of increased interest and support for day-care in other church denominations that recognize the importance of establishing quality day-care in their communities. I read of Mennonite voluntary service workers who are off to work in day-care centers for various groups all over North America. This is a valuable service, but what about our own children? As a Mennonite people we have traditionally been very concerned about education. We pour a great deal of money each year into support of Mennonite high schools and colleges and more recently elementary schools and even universities. What about Mennonite day-cares and nursery schools? The first five years are the most important and influential years in the child's life. In these five years his or her learning capabilities, attitudes, and social behaviors are shaped and moulded. Yet during these crucial years we seem the least concerned for our children's education.

In spite of minimal resources our day-care does manage to provide quality care that we are happy with. Our son has many friends there. The children go on field trips, have interesting visitors, participate in daily arts and crafts activities, go to the gym twice a week, are exposed to stories, music and poetry and have many play experiences that wouldn't normally be provided at home. Most of the time we are satisfied that the amount of extra time and money we invest in the day-care is worth it.

I love my work as a teacher. I feel that in teaching I can best put to use the talents I have been given. I love my work as a mother and cannot imagine life without our son who has brought untold joy, fulfillment, and meaning to our lives. Working at two demanding and rewarding full-time jobs has not always been easy, but I am convinced that it is the right thing for me and my family at this time in our lives.

Mary Lou Driedger teaches Grade 1 in Steinbach, Manitoba.

Chapter 5
LeARNiNg TO live WiTh disAbiliTies

by Carol Friesen

Another C-section. I am scheduled for January 4, 1967. After anaesthesia (a spinal block) I lie down, my head lower than the rest of my body, so my baby can be delivered. When the baby appears from the incision, Dr. Janzen works for what seems eternity suctioning him, trying to get him to breathe. Finally he cries out.

Another boy! Chad Jonathan. But I will not be able to hold him for six days. Instead when I am finally up to it the next day, LeRoy and I walk to the window to see our baby boy struggling to breathe, in an isolette with oxygen. During the night he has had increasing difficulty breathing. For three days he labors with breathing. Later Dr. Janzen tells me that if he had not been eight pounds and six ounces we would have lost him.

I go home with LeRoy on the third day. I have not yet been able to hold my baby—I cannot claim him until I finally return on the sixth day to try and nurse him. Finally he is my baby. I hold him and snuggle him, checking him over carefully.

While I have been at home he has developed jaundice. A decision needs to be made about the need for an exchange transfusion. We wait. His bilirubin begins to go down. No transfusion. . . relief.

Finally he is nine days old. We can take him home. Those first years he is developing normally, crawling, walking, talking, like any other baby. I feel I should know. After all I have spent the past five years working in pediatrics and see children at all stages of development. But there's a nagging feeling. Why are breakfasts so messy? Why after he has learned to walk does he bump things so much? It is a nagging feeling that is always there but somehow I soothe myself by saying he is just more clumsy. Once in a while LeRoy asks, "But why does he seem better after he has had breakfast?" The questions persist.

When Chad is three years old I take him to Dr. Maxwell in Iowa City. "Dr. Maxwell," I say, "my child is clumsy. He seems to be better after eating breakfast. My father is a diabetic. My niece was two years old when she became diabetic. Is he becoming diabetic?" The doctor checks him carefully, doing the necessary testing. I am not satisfied. I return again. I do not remember how often I return before he finally sends us to the University of Iowa Hospital School for further testing.

When all the testing is done, LeRoy and I sit down with the doctor. He tells us, "Your child has some brain damage but the problem is not progressive. He will probably have to learn to type because he will not be able to write. There is damage to the fine movements. He probably will have a slight gait problem as well. He is intelligent. It has not affected his intelligence."

Relief! It is not progressive. We can learn to live with this. We share all this with our small group from church. He will not be mentally retarded.

When Chad is four years old we accept an assignment with the Mennonite Central Committee to live in Jerusalem. This will mean that Chad will begin school there. Kindergarten goes well. Writing is not involved to a great extent. We relax.

But Fran Eriksen, another international volunteer, says that we really need to see a neurologist because she sees some problems with Chad. She has had years of experience in physical therapy with disabled children. So we begin our visits to the neurologist, Dr. Amir. Because of what she sees in the electroencephalogram she is amazed that Chad is not having convulsions. But she does not tell me this until later.

Learning to Live with Disabilities

On our way to the United States for furlough, we spend five weeks traveling in Europe. Little do we know that this will be the last summer we will be able to travel with Chad without a wheelchair. We enjoy our travels as a family that summer very much.

After our furlough we return to Lebanon to a village outside of Beirut. All three children are accepted into Catholic schools. The teacher understands that Chad cannot write and works with him in class.

In February of 1975 LeRoy returns to Jerusalem for a scheduled visit. While he is there Chad develops a fever and probable ear infection. The children and I travel the forty-five-minute taxi drive into Beirut to see the pediatrician. He takes a history of Chad before the physical exam. When I tell him about Chad's delivery, his respiratory disease after birth, and his problems now, he takes a piece of paper, asks Chad to come and draw a person. Chad, eight years old, draws a person with fingers and toes, eyes, ears, hair, etc. The doctor looks at me, relieved, and says the problem is due to his respiratory disease but he has good intelligence. At least that is not affected! He then checks his ears—yes, another ear infection. Treatment begins.

I am angry that the doctor is so matter-of-fact. As long as his intelligence is not affected, all is well. All is not well! Soon a pattern begins. About an hour after Chad falls asleep he begins to wail out. Sometimes it is a "Mo-o-m. . . " that trails off. By the time we get to his bed, he is fast asleep. He is breathing all right. We sigh and go to our room. But this persists. Then one evening I realize he is a little blue. I ask myself, "What is happening?" I do not realize that he is having a convulsion.

An appointment is made with the neurologist at Beirut University. Chad sits there while I describe his convulsions. The doctor prescribes Dilantin and we go home.

On the way home Chad says to me, "Mom, why don't you tell me what is happening to me at night? I want to know." He has sat through that whole visit with the doctor and listened to me tell the doctor things about him which he did not know. After that I work at keeping him informed about

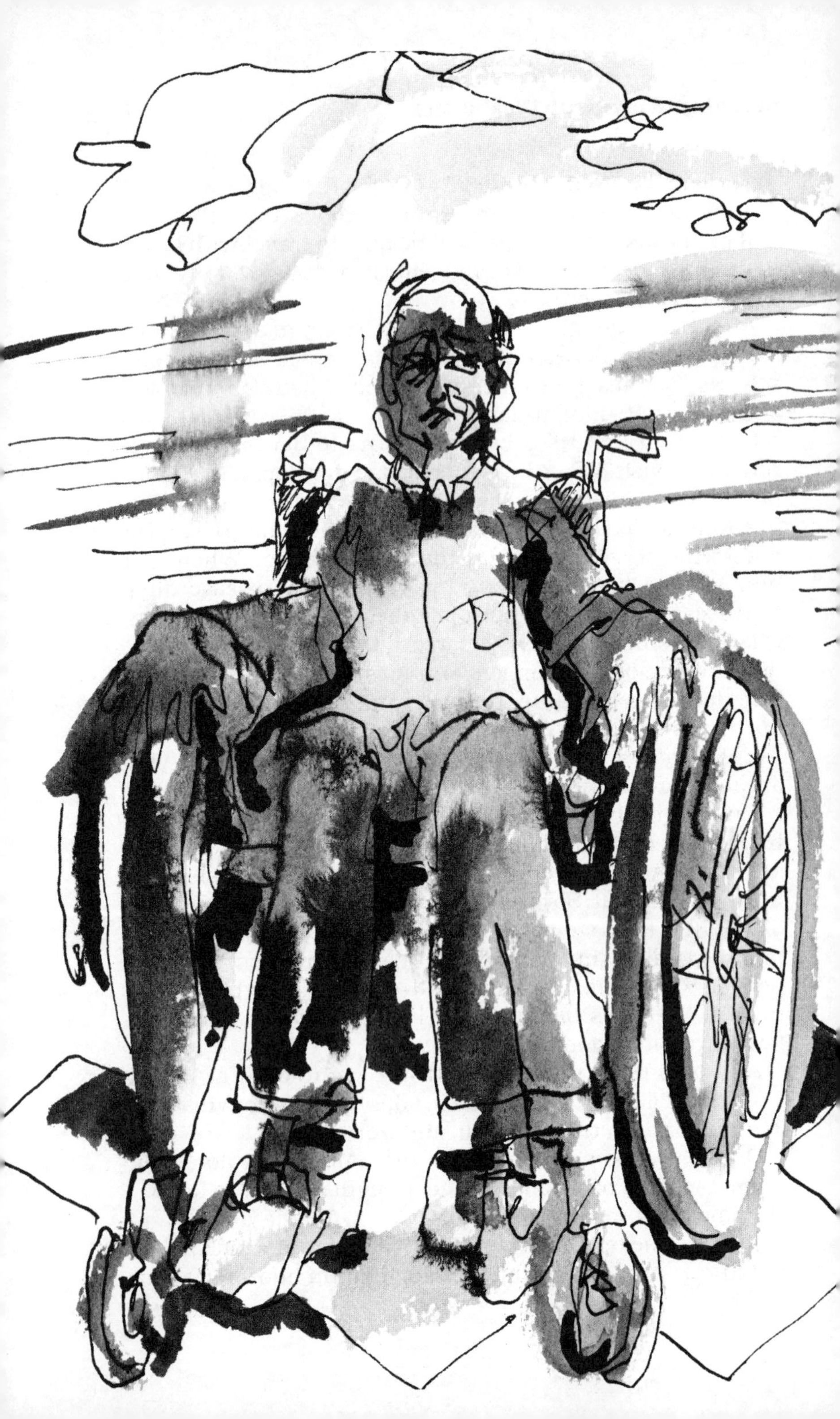

Learning to Live with Disabilities

what is happening.

Shortly after we begin the medicine, his coordination begins to get worse. One day when he goes to the bathroom, we rush to him as we hear him bouncing between the fixtures. We begin helping him in the bathroom. His eating becomes messier. He has more trouble dressing himself. He no longer can tie his shoes. There are visits to the doctor, medicine changes. The convulsions continue.

That March the civil war begins in Lebanon. Often fighting is going on between us and Beirut. We cannot reach the doctor when we need to, even on the phone. We spend more time at home because of the troubles. Our tragedy and Lebanon's tradegy flow into each other. Often we are numb. Sometimes we cry. Often we are angry. But at whom, at what?

The end of June comes. One night Chad has the worst convulsion he has ever had. I give him artificial respiration. Finally he begins to breathe and his color returns. I give a big sigh and say to LeRoy, "Let's get back to Jerusalem where the doctor is available." The next morning we begin to pack and get rid of things we do not want to take with us. On Monday when LeRoy calls the U.S. Embassy to say we are leaving via Damascus, they tell us we cannot leave because there is heavy fighting along the road in the Bekas Valley between us and Damascus. The next day we risk it and leave anyway. Five people are never as relieved as when we cross the border into Syria.

It is a relief to be back with Dr. Amir, the neurologist. She changes some of Chad's medicines and soon the convulsions are further apart—sometimes ten days apart. But Chad gets more "shaky." One day he cannot keep his balance. He has to crawl to get to his bedroom. He and LeRoy sit and cry together that day. There will be many more times like this. There still are.

Dr. Amir does all sorts of testing that year. She sends us to Hadassah Hospital. Finally in the spring of 1976 she looks at me and says, "I have nothing else to offer you. I have exhausted the resources here in Israel. I would encourage you to go back to the United States where a lot of research is being done. Perhaps they will find something to help Chad."

We are very bruised people as we return to the United States. We have experienced the tragedy of our child along with the tragedy of the Middle East.

We locate with a church community that has invited us. This had been our first church home after marriage so it is like a homecoming. People ask about Chad and we talk.

At first Chad has no trouble getting friends. He has a three-wheel bike. Friends come. He is fun to play with. But boys his age begin enjoying sports for competition and winning. Chad cannot compete. He is courageous and when given time he stands wobbly at the plate, grasping the bat and swinging. Sometimes he manages to hit the ball. But then he falls. His legs just will not do what he wants and the ball is thrown to the first baseman before he starts for first base. Clumsy! Clumsy feelings—how sad...how courageous...how outrageous...why? Why our son? With all his courage he would be quite a sportsman. We are filled with pain and grief.

My friends say they do not know how I do it. Do what? He is my son. I love him. What else can I do?

In Jerusalem Madame Berreby tutored Chad and kept him at grade level with A's and B's. But here in the United States, first one year goes by and then another and I find teachers relying on testing, on workbooks, and missing what Chad has to offer and where his strengths are. Will anyone else see what I see in him? Am I crazy? Am I denying something? Can't my child learn? Why can't he read? More questions. More and more answers such as, "I do not know," "I do not have any more help for you," "There is no diagnosis, therefore no prognosis."

Chad has friends living close enough to visit on his bike. But fewer and fewer friends return his visits without being invited.

Society tells us in order to be human one must be intelligent, strong, athletic. I have found humanity with Chad and some of his friends in school when I saw little elsewhere: the child who speaks few words but remembers my name and hugs me when she sees me; Chad's friend who tells me of his

Learning to Live with Disabilities

parents' separation but asks me not to tell Chad because it would hurt him too much; Chad's companions in special education who participate in special olympics with canes, braces, and wheelchairs. In spite of falling or coming in last, each one finishes the race she or he has entered.

Friends have reached out to me in many ways. The last year in Jerusalem, Anny Yoder kept Chad overnight at least one weekend a month. Did she realize what that was for me, sharing my nightly fear of awakening to hear Chad convulsing? Did she know how she helped me carry my pain that year by choosing to care in this way?

Friends have listened to me many hours as I tried to talk through my agony of how I could help this boy live life to the fullest. There was a lot of affirming. There was helpful advice. There was discussion. Friends helped me struggle with many questions. What is a full life? Does having good grades, being able to graduate mean fullness of life? What if your brother and sister seem to accomplish what they decide to do? And you lie there dreaming of driving a car or being a star baseball player but knowing you never will.

We have been fortunate because there have been other adults in our church settings who made efforts to include Chad in activities for his age. As Chad has gotten older and into his teens the pain has been more with how he works with feeling included by his peers. We are grateful for those who include him, but it is sometimes a real test because Chad needs physical help. For teenagers, becoming independent is much of their emotional work. How do we help Chad in this journey when he depends on us for his physical needs? What does independence mean for him? It seems difficult enough for us to help teenagers who do not need to consider physical dependence through these years. Many times other teenagers have enough to cope with on their own journey and being with Chad is too difficult for them. This is painful because even though I understand, Chad still is left alone.

The children in church (most of our social life has centered in church) have taught Chad and us a lot. Chad and I talked about this. All of a sudden he would experience being left out and not knowing what he had done (or thinking it was something he had done). We would discover it had to do with the fact that he was physically handicapped, could not always walk straight and needed assistance, needed help eating, etc. This had become a barrier. But why?

One day I picked up Harold H. Wilke's book, *Creating the Caring Congregation*. He described clearly what we had been experiencing and trying to talk about. Chad's friends, both children and adults, were having some emotional responses which were very real. These responses were based on fears not fully realized:

> My first fear is that somehow this disability of the other individual is catching. It might actually infect me. As soon as I say this in words, I recognize how foolish the concept is, but the fear, usually unconscious to me, is actually present.
>
> A second fear is related to the first; this unknown thing out there attached to this person is threatening to me in still other ways. I do not understand how the threat exists; I only know that I am afraid. The person with the obvious handicap represents the unknown, and I am scared of the unknown. . .
>
> The third fear is more agonizing, because it represents something that is actually in me; it symbolizes my own weakness and my own inability. It makes me cry out in recognition of my own handicaps and my own shortcomings. In this case, the fear is not something created by that thing out there, it is what that thing actually induces within me, so that I am now torn within myself.
>
> When I see someone who is severely crippled, my fears respond to this inner anxiety about the vulnerability, the shortcomings and handicaps existing within myself.
>
> "The kingdom of God is not complete without the poor and maimed." And each member thereof is not complete, or has hope of salvation unless his own lameness or her own blindness, the negative aspects of their lives, are included.[1]

Sympathy is not something we need. We need "empathy."

It includes the ability to walk the very narrow line between swamping a newly bereaved or handicapped person with concern and affection and leaving him entirely alone out of fear of invasion of privacy or concern for our own embarrassment. We need to be seen as participants rather than recipients of service.

Before Chad, before the Middle East, before war, before. . . I did not know about Good Friday and Easter, about death and resurrection. Only when I had experienced death could I experience resurrection. Only after I had experienced black Friday could I experience bright Easter Sunday morning with "He is risen, risen indeed." Only because I have experienced darkness and death can I experience life—the resurrection. The story of Jesus and his life makes sense to me. Sense? Well, how else can I say all this except that this is my experience? If God had not been with me through each step of this path, I could not believe today, and that would be living death. God's word to me has been life: That you may know him and the power of his resurrection.

Carol Friesen works as a registered nurse in Elkhart, Indiana, and is studying part-time at the Mennonite Biblical Seminary.

NOTES
[1]*Creating the Caring Congregation: Guidelines for Ministering with the Handicapped.* Nashville, Tenn.: Abingdon, 1980.

Chapter 6
SEARCHING FOR SHALOM IN MENNONITE ATHLETICS

by Del Glick

"Open your eyes, you blind zebra," yells an irate spectator above the noise of the crowd. "Can't you see she was fouled?"

"Victory in Jesus" sing a happy group of athletes after a last-second come-from-behind win. They ignore the dejected faces of their opponents.

"Make sure you don't have three ladies in the same row," an adult male advises the person in charge of organizing the volleyball game.

"Kill, kill, kill," chants a group of hyped-up high school soccer players on their way to the athletic field.

The spectators stand en masse looking at the flag during the playing of the national anthem and then heartily join in singing, "God Bless America." Quietly and reverently they bow their heads as a local minister leads in the opening prayer.

"Push 'em back, push 'em back, way back," shouts a group of short-skirted blond and brunette girls as they jump up and down cheering on "their guys."

"You are the worst coach I ever saw. Damn it, what gives you the right not to play my son?" The phone clicks as the angry parent hangs up.

The basketball player slams the ball down hard after what

Searching for Shalom in Mennonite Athletics

he thinks was a bad call. "Technical foul," indicates the official.

"Boo-oo-oo," yell the spectators.

"I was in the net," admits the teenager playing on an intergenerational church volleyball team.

"No, you weren't," disagrees a teammate twice his age.

"Yes, I was," retorts the youth.

After an intense argument, the teenager mutters, "And to think he calls himself a member of this church and wants me to be dishonest!"

In the world of athletics such scenes are commonplace. But in this case, they are real-life examples and situations of Mennonites involved in athletics!

My personal interest in recreation and sports goes back to my rearing on a farm in central Pennsylvania. While work was a priority, play was important for our family. My parents took time from their busy schedule to play with us four children.

High school involvements increased my liking for athletics and, while studying at a Mennnonite college, I had several opportunities to coach both male and female intramural teams. My fascination and enjoyment of coaching persisted and led me to serve as athletic director and coach at two Mennonite high schools during the next seven years. My experiences included coaching junior high, freshmen, junior varsity and varsity—boys and girls—in soccer, basketball, softball, and track and field.

During my initial years of coaching in a Mennonite setting, something deep within began troubling me. How should Mennonites/Anabaptists do athletics and recreation? My observations indicated that most Mennonites do not approach sports any differently than others do. My uneasiness and ongoing search finally crystallized into this conclusion: as Mennonites, we have been taught that nonresistant love is a central ingredient of our faith and heritage. But no one has ever told us that being a peacemaker has anything to do with recreation and sports! With that realization, I felt sadness and disappointment. I was impressed with the creative and innovative programming Mennonites had done with peace education in school and church curricula. I appreciated the way Mennonites revitalized the peace emphasis in view of escalating military spending and the pending draft. But why had Mennonites not consciously, adequately, or systematically incorporated their historic peacemaking values into their athletics? Where was direction and guidance in this area which affects so many of us Mennonites?

If the peacemaking/shalom dimensions of our faith do not constitute the theological and practical framework and foundation out of which Mennonites do athletics, then I question the validity of our being involved with it. Athletics and the shalom motif cannot be divorced from each other. If they are, we have either an inappropriate theology or an inadequate pastime.

Shalom is a rich biblical concept in which the personhood of every individual is uplifted. It defines the good life of wholeness, well-being, and salvation as a responsive individual in covenant community with God. There is no peace with one's neighbor unless there is mutual care and responsibility for all neighbors.

Shalom united the concern for individual well-being with the needs of the whole community. The individual achieves his or her personal fulfillment within the context of the whole human family and community. Shalom does not destroy or violate maleness or femaleness but rather affirms their creation in the image and likeness of God.

Furthermore, as Jack L. Stotts writes in his book *Shalom: The Search for a Peaceable City*, "Peacemaking in all its richness and complexity becomes an ongoing and initiatory activity, not just a reaction to defects in relationships. It contradicts all those human practices and institutions that disfigure life."[1] The well-being, harmony, mutual care, responsibility, and accountability of a shalom community can be felt.

What are some implications of shalom in Mennonite athletics?

(1) *We do not participate in athletics with a win-at-all-*

Searching for Shalom in Mennonite Athletics 47

cost attitude. We dare not become like Vince Lombardi whose professional football philosophy was: "Winning isn't everything; it's the only thing." Neither can we reflect what one Mennonite high school coach said recently, "What's all this stuff about peacemaking? The only thing I'm concerned about is winning." Responsible recreation calls for desire, concentration, and hard work with the overarching goal of playing up to one's potential. In such a framework the final score is not as important as how one plays the game.

Yet we Mennonites find ourselves in a culture where winning has become a primary means for getting praise and attention and defeat is considered ample reason for shame and guilt. Unfortunately, even the gospel message itself is often distorted by promising success to those who profess faith. Such an emphasis leaves an athlete without a biblical concept of God if defeat occurs.

All that is caught up in the winning motif must be taken in proper perspective in shalom athletics. Teamwork must be highlighted while individual rewards and trophies are downplayed or at best eliminated. Typical media coverage should give way to alternatives emphasizing cooperation and personhood. The usual militarism and emotionalism of pep rallies that advocate winning for the sake of winning have no place in shalom communities.

Shalom does not measure success by the number of wins or losses, or points scored, but by how many times athletes have played and lived up to their peacemaking potential—physically, emotionally, mentally, and spiritually. After all, the cross gives no promise of manageable success. The call to follow is not one to effectiveness but to faithfulness.

(2) *We recognize competition as having both negative and positive qualities.* The "competition debate" has been around for a long time. According to some, competition is all bad; others suggest that competition is inherent in human nature and if guided can be beneficial.

The fact that humans show competitive feelings at a very early age (and before cooperative feelings emerge) indicates a continuing need for an activity through which one may learn to handle competitive feelings. Yet a high school sophomore may reflect the feelings of many Mennonites: "I'm so sick of the athletic scene. . . when the level of competition becomes so intense that the players turn on each other, it's time to put an end to the whole mess. I always thought the purpose of playing sports was to have some fun. . . but the number of inferiority complexes and shattered confidences is great."[2]

It is my opinion that athletics does not necessarily increase competiton. There appears to be as much, if not more, competition taking place in a school classroom or among leadership personnel of a congregation as there is on the basketball court. Competitive persons often get into athletics, but athletics does not automatically produce competitive persons. The suffering servant motif and the concept of peoplehood well known in Mennonite circles often seems to be dichotomous to the nature of organized competitive athletics. But it certainly does not have to be. Shalom athletics calls for guidance and direction of the gift of competitiveness given to us by our Creator.

(3) *We view sportsmanship as definitive, not optional.* It is sad to observe church members who the night before were bad-mouthing officials, players, and coaches piously worshiping on a Sunday morning. It is disappointing to see Mennonite athletes lose their cool in the midst of an athletic context. It is disgusting to witness Mennonite coaches go storming onto the court to argue with the referee. It is upsetting to hear cheers or slogans which advocate, "Fight, fight, fight," or suggest smashing/beating/stomping the other team.

Participants of shalom athletics look for positive ways to relate to each other in wholeness as human beings. To downgrade another person, including one's opponent, by action, words, or blame is to destroy shalom. Mennonite brothers and sisters need to be able to affirm and cheer for good plays on both teams; to appreciate the efforts of the officials; to encourage players and coaches, and to work hard for the well-being of all persons involved. It is difficult to remain under control and discipline when the competition is close, especially when a family member or close friend is playing. It is not easy to keep calm when not everything is being noticed by the officials. It is tempting to join others around you in booing or expressing anger and hostility. But being peacemakers in the bleachers or on the court is as important as being peacemakers in the congregation or on the mission field.

(4) *We strive for equal regard, mutuality, and wholeness of male and female.* The oppressive stereotypes of masculinity and femininity that emerge in and often pervade the area of sports need to be abolished. Shalom athletics does not have any room for hyped-up short-skirted cute chicks doing sexy routines in an attempt to get more fans cheering for the super male jocks out on the court or field.

Shalom athletics guards against the deterioration and destruction of the personhood of male and female. It encourages coed involvement whenever possible. It seeks for equal budgeting, recognition, and priority. It implements creative cheering alternatives. It provides involvement for many, not only a chosen few. It calls into question highly organized sports whose objectives and rules allow for the hitting or blocking of other human beings, e.g., football, ice hockey, and boxing. It is sensitive to the needs and gifts of all participants. It perpetuates individual and community self-worth. It eliminates all sexism.

Male and female were created in the image and likeness of God. Anything that does not honor that creation model is less than shalom.

(5) *We resist the temptation of a God-Country-Athletics theology.* The temptation of combining and interweaving God, country, and athletics represents a strange paradox and process. While such a happening is most clearly evident in the professional ranks of athletics, it affects all of us. This temptation does not push God out of the picture completely; rather, it is a subtle, zealous, and idolatrous attempt to link Christianity with athletics. It becomes a blending and often an unconscious blurring of the two kingdoms—the kingdom of this world and the kingdom of God.

In this popular "born-again" era, it is advantageous for

the athlete to be "Christian." After all, if God is on the side of the Christian athlete, then victory should be automatic. Popular Christian magazines and organizations like the Fellowship of Christian Athletes usually share only stories of the successful, faithful, and pietistic athlete. What is forgotten is that God is not the God of success but the God of faithfulness. God is much bigger than our victories and defeats.

Furthermore, nationalism and patriotism have no place in shalom athletics. This does not indicate a lack of respect or honor for our country, but such a stance clearly portrays and affirms that there is only one God who is worthy of our allegiance, and that God is not the God of athletics or the God of nationalism.

God calls us first to be followers of Jesus on the way. God's kingdom receives priority. All involvements, including athletics, are secondary. You cannot serve God and athletics. You cannot worship God and the golden calf of sports. We only participate in athletics to develop our personalities and to use the gifts our Creator has given to us. Consequently, the wedding of sports and God and country can never take place in shalom athletics.

I believe sports can be valid, appropriate, necessary, yet I have observed firsthand some of its crippling and devastating effects on Mennonites. The issue for me is not should we/should we not, but rather how, when, and to what degree. From the pick-up sandlot dynamic to more informally organized recreation, from grade school through college and church leagues, the principles of shalom need to be realized through our participation in athletics. This is an ongoing process which I hope will keep on giving birth to new dimensions in being brothers and sisters in God's shalom community.

Del Glick co-pastors Waterford Mennonite Church in Goshen, Indiana, with his wife, Charlotte Glick.

NOTES

[1] New York: Abingdon Press, 1973, p. 202.
[2] Edward R. Walsh, "Sporting Blood," *The Rotarian* (June 1976), pp. 18-20.

Chapter 7
UNdERSTANdiNG SEXUALiTY

by Keith C. Schrag

Sex and sexuality are areas that were not talked about as I was growing up in the Mennonite church. Even saying the words was uncomfortable for both speaker and listener. As a result I have found it quite difficult to work through a personal understanding of sex and sexuality in my life.

Like anger, loneliness, and discouragement, sex is scary to explore and talk about. The fear of failing or of doing something awful and irreparable is deeply ingrained within me. I find it much more comfortable to give the traditionally supported answers, black and white, than to deal in depth with the dilemmas that are beyond those easy answers. But the only way I have found to grow as a human being is to accept God's promise to be with me wherever I go and to struggle or forge ahead on the pioneering trail leading to fuller understanding of my sexuality.

Sexuality encompasses a broad area. It includes my need to be with other people, my awareness of myself as a person and as a being in relationship with other human beings, my need to be unique and separate from other persons, and my relationship with the totality of creation and the Creator.

Sexuality starts with and includes my need to affirm myself and appreciate myself. I have had difficulty doing this. I learned "not to think too highly of myself" (Rom. 12:3b), but I was not taught the skill of "thinking with a sober estimate of myself" (Rom: 12:3c). In church settings I have been so warned against conceit that I have responded with a deep hesitancy to affirm the God-given gifts and abilities that I have.

One area that needs developing in the church is an adequate theology of sexuality. In the past few years I have been able to read some papers that have not been available openly in the denomination, papers from peers in the pastorate that have written some reflections or studies on sexuality, papers from the Mennonite Medical Association, Young Adult seminars, and articles from MCC's Peace Section Task Force on Women in Church and Society. These resources have been quite helpful, but they have been made available cautiously and with the awareness that they do not represent a "denominational point of view." The church has been most hesitant to say anything publicly about sexuality. So our theology of sexuality remains largely undefined or nonexistent.

A few persons have worked in other denominations to develop helpful aids in the search for a clear biblical and theological understanding. One such person whose work I've found most beneficial is James B. Nelson in his book *Embodiment* (Minneapolis: Augsburg, 1978). Nelson indicates that we have considered the body as bad and the spirit as good—a borrowing from Hellenism rather than a Hebrew understanding of the body. My experiences support his claim; I have learned that it is a temple of the Holy Spirit, but I have not been taught to enjoy my body. The enjoyment I am learning is in direct contrast to the fear of pleasure and the stigma attached to pleasuring that I acquired from my earlier mentors.

Touching, a particularly healing ministry that Jesus emphasized so much, has not been part of my church experience. Although I observed the kiss of charity (or holy kiss) as a youngster, I decided then that I was not going to engage in that unsanitary and suspect practice! Foot washing, another ritual experience of touch within our tradition, has largely fallen into disrepute among many younger Mennonites. Yet, we need occasions for touching each other and for being touched by others.

I was excited some time ago to find an article in our local newspaper that indicated studies show that we need at least eight hugs a day. I made good use of that! I have enjoyed and

Understanding Sexuality

appreciated the increasing chances, both in church settings and otherwise, to hug and to experience the warmth of human closeness. We need to encourage warm interchanges in our church.

Sexuality, according to Genesis and other scriptural teaching, is part of the Lord's intention for us from the beginning. We are created as body-beings, persons that think, feel, decide. We are composed of minds, hearts, souls, and bodies. We have a more highly developed theology or statement of doctrine about the first three, both formally and informally defined, than the last. We have yet to develop the understanding in the church that the body is a most honorable creation that has been given us to explore and steward. Our embarrassment about the Song of Solomon indicates this uncomfortableness. Rather than taking its sensuous language and imagery literally, the church has usually spiritualized the meaning of this book.

Although we believe that the body as we know it does not go with our spirit at our death, we are not merely souls that are trapped in bodies until the Spirit in mercy releases us from this terrible condition! Thank God, no. We have been given these glorious tents in which we dwell and which become (or can become) for us a means to understand in greater depth the mysteries of God and of creation. My anger, my loneliness, my sadness, my despair, my dissatisfaction, my fear, my sensuality, my compassion, my longing to grow, my seeking for community—all are tremendous gifts to me that God, in great wisdom, has given for me to steward.

I need the church and the resources of the church—its literature, its persons in official capacity, its settings of worship and retreat, its brothers and sisters—to be co-pilgrims with me in this scary and marvelous journey to wholeness. I need to discover my sexuality and to steward it in order to progress on that journey. The Lord has called me to seek for wholeness. To refuse that would be to renege on my call to be a faithful disciple and would deny the power of the Spirit to enable me in my weakness.

Our conspiracy of silence in the church (sex as a hush-

hush subject) has left me with little sense of understanding about many of the aspects of sex and sexuality. I have picked up many of these by private reading of Song of Solomon with its sensuous language and imagery, in settings of clinical training (like my Clinical Pastoral Education experience at a Mennonite-related mental health center), and through street language discovered in inner city ministries and other areas often labeled evil by our religious structures. I have been grateful for these experiences and I want to share this learning with my brothers and sisters in appropriate settings and ways. Yet, when I have sought to do this through churchwide channels there has been response of appreciation for the concern but unwillingness to "open that can of worms."

In some young adult settings, however, I have found that there are persons, older and younger, who have been isolated for many years with their haunting questions and with deep pains that they have kept only to themselves. For these they have found no resources within the church, by and large, for sharing and for healing and growing.

One area that can help us as we grow is to accept the language and terms of *sex* and *sexuality* as being amoral. Just as we see words like *house* and *car* as being without good or bad value judgment, so also are words like *penis*, *vagina*, and *intercourse*. We have developed a sense that such words should not be used in public.

Is the experience of sex and being sexual persons really one of shame, rather than of God-given enjoyment and opportunity (as well as responsibility)? I recall the shock some people expressed at hearing the words *penis* and *vagina* in a church worship setting when the pastor was talking about male/femaleness. It reminded me that most of our church experience has not included such language. Since we only feel good about those aspects of ourselves that we can talk about, we need to grow in loving our whole selves and in affirming all parts of our bodies.

Early in life I learned that sex had to do with intercourse and that that was reserved for two people who were married to each other. Once, when I was barely a teenager, a young friend a year older than I came to our home to talk with my father, the pastor of our congregation. The girl's mother came with her. From the tears and somberness of the occasion I knew something awful had happened. Later I realized what it was. The girl married her young boyfriend, after making a confession in church. The heaviness of this situation was increased by the air of secrecy surrounding it. This remained with me and underscored the many times I was to hear, in church settings, that we are to be careful with the evil passions that surge within us. It was impressed deeply within me that sex was sacred and could only be understood and experienced within a Christian marriage and that we must firmly control the unruly, eruptive forces inside us. The language used communicated fear and judgment. The lack of candid discussion taught me that Christians should not talk or even think about such things! This plagued me during my adolescent and early adult years. The church, rather than being an effective help (as it really intended to be) had been another barrier to growth and wholeness.

The fear of sex and of sexuality still lurks within me, even though I have worked hard revising these early misconceptions. Some of the revising has been with the help of the church, but most of it has been apart from the church and often with the awareness that this area is still one which is not talked about. ("The good Christian knows what the Bible teaches and what God demands about sex and lives in obedience to that command," is the essence of teaching I generally hear among Mennonites.)

This is far from adequate. Not only do I need much more; many of the people with whom I interact also need more. Young adults and older persons often ask for help but are told the church is not yet ready to deal openly with this subject.

I have felt caught in the middle of this tension. I have had numerous opportunities to work at the issues that confront me personally and that face my brothers and sisters. I have continued to work as I could to bring within the settings of the church the chance to look together to find options that make sense to Christians who are seeking to be obedient to the teaching of Christ and honest with themselves and each other. Often this has been in settings with younger adults. Usually, however, it has been with considerable caution since the risk of being misunderstood is high.

In spite of the risks, we need to minister to ourselves and to each other in ways that will reflect the ministry and teachings of Christ and will deal pastorally and creatively with our expressed needs. One way to work at this, as a start, is to look at key terms, develop an understanding of them, and become comfortable with them.

Some terms relating to sexuality beg for clarification. While words like *commitment* and *covenant* are often used, along with *relationship, marriage, family, singleness, divorce,* and *remarriage,* terms like *intimacy, sexual orientation,* and other expressions relating to sexuality tend not to be discussed openly. Perhaps this reflects our lack of understanding and acquaintance since embarrassment and indications of condemnation often accompany use of these terms.

Intimacy is a component of sexuality that is often misunderstood. If we are to be intimate with God we need to learn what intimacy means within our human interactions. Intimacy is more than merely sexual intimacy. Intellectual, aesthetic, work, and fun activities are all occasions of intimacy. Intimacy, at this point, is sharing of myself and my interests with another human being in a way that discloses something about myself and receives some level of disclosure from the other. The level of intimacy, the depth, and the permanence depend on the covenant we have with each other. The deepest intimacy I share with my wife, and that is the most permanent of all my interpersonal commitments. Yet, I am intimate at some level with many people. It takes many persons to meet my intimacy needs. Some years ago I heard the observation made that as a married person I can only realistically expect my spouse to meet 20 percent of my intimacy needs. That shocked me at first. I am more aware now that our joint friends, my peers in both ministry and counseling, my personal friends and persons with whom I interact in other aspects of my daily living give me many occasions for intimate contact.

Closely related to intimacy is the concern for *reciprocity* and *mutuality* of the shared experiences and support. I'm continually testing what I choose to share or risk, how the receiver might receive it, and how much is appropriate in the particular setting. To give full vent to my yearnings or fears might be quite destructive since it would cause both recipient and me to recoil in confusion and fear. My vulnerability and openness in disclosures need to be tempered by the boundaries appropriate to that relationship at that time. The question of mutual commitment and my friend's level of availability and responsiveness to me are crucial in determining how much I disclose about my hopes, pains, fears, and fantasies.

The church has given a few general rules and prohibitions. We are taught as Christians to love each other, to bear each other's burdens, to confess our sins to each other, to forgive each other, to restore each other. We are told not to kill, not to judge, not to gossip, not to hurt. These are most important aspects of human relationships and to Christian community building. We need further guidance, however, in the particulars of our circumstances, in the day-by-day aspects of love and forgiveness. We also need each other's help in working through the problems and questions that arise as we work at being intimate with each other, at the closeness and distance needs, the boundaries, of our relationships.

We also need to discuss our fears with others—fears of being overwhelmed, fears of being rejected, fears of losing control, fears of disclosing too much, fears of our fantasies, fears of being worthless. We need to talk about loneliness and yearnings for completeness. We need to find ways to share together with others about self-image—our concern about attractions to others, about whether or not we are attractive. The church is created to be a community, the people of God. Therefore, we need to deal with the issues that are basic to that community-ness. Our merger with others and our separation from others, what draws us to intimacy and what pushes us to isolation, are of tremendous importance.

We need to talk more in the church about what *fidelity* means and to be more clear about *sexual exclusiveness* in our relationships. What do both terms mean? Why are they significant to us, to our relationships, to the community? A blanket prohibition has not been adequate for me; I have had to seek in other-than-Mennonite settings for most of my help in understanding the deeper aspects of fidelity and sexual exclusiveness. Generally, the church (regardless of denomination) has been hesitant to deal with this issue. Are these two different issues or does fidelity automatically mean sexual exclusiveness? Why or why not? Before we quickly answer, let's look at the deeper questions. Are the biblical instructions timeless or are there particular aspects of both Old Testament and New Testament teachings that relate uniquely to their specific cultures and thus need to be considered in greater depth before drawing simple parallels in application to our situations? We need further help in working together, hearing from those who do not agree with us as well as those who do, in this area.

Sex is another term that needs clarification. *Sex* is a broad term, often used to refer only to the genital aspects of our sexuality. But sex relates to my being male/female, to my being a sexual person, and to the way I choose to express my sexuality. *Genital sex* is the term I choose to use in reference to sexual activity between persons that is expressed in ways that include genital arousal, usually through some contact with the genital organs, and often including orgasm. Genital sex also includes masturbation. Since *sex* refers to such a broad spectrum we do well to state specifically when we mean *genital* sex. Again, our genital organs, both those exposed and those within the body, are all given as God's good creation. It is important that we learn to receive and talk about them without a false sense of shame.

Homosexuality refers to that aspect of us which is attracted to persons of the same gender. It refers both to attractions and orientation and to activity. The Kinsey report of 1963 indicated that on a scale of 0 (exclusively heterosexual in orientation) to 6 (exclusively homosexual) most of us are along the continuum somewhere between the two extremes. Persons with equal attraction and/or genital sexual experience to both genders are 3, on the scale, for example.

Other psychologists, Jung, for instance, refer to the anima/animus within us. When God created us human, God created us male and female, with aspects of that combination being expressed within all of us. We can only understand ourselves, offer that of ourselves to God, and serve God in committed obedience, as we develop an acceptance and awareness of what it means to be created as male/female/ or as female/male—in God's image.

Homophobia is the fear of homosexuality and of persons who are homosexual. This fear can be expressed in an unwillingness to look at or deal with persons who are gay, in unwillingness to look at the homosexual sensibilities within ourselves, in our violence through hurtful words and deeds toward gay people. I believe the church has a great need to deal with its homophobia. The exclusion of gay men and lesbians is evidence to me of a judgment and condemnation that Jesus refused to be part of. (The New Testament contains no such teaching of Jesus, at any rate, and is most consistent in its reporting that Jesus showed compassion, especially toward those condemned by religious people.) The church in general has not been helpful to me in understanding homosexuality or homophobia. The issue is too controversial to deal with, the church has often said. However, many brothers and sisters have asked for help, have offered help, and have indicated the need to deal redemptively and openly with homosexuality. I experience the failure to do so as sin since it further alienates us from each other and even from ourselves.

The terms *gay* and *lesbian* are preferable to *homosexual* for many persons. *Homosexual* tends to refer more to the component of sexuality and not the relational and orientation aspects. *Gay* is the term people tend to prefer when they have accepted their sexual orientation. Currently *gay* is often used to refer to all homosexual people, but it is more specifically used to refer to males. *Lesbian* is the preferred term for females. Our language can be used as a bridge or a wall in relationships. I experience that using the terms *gay* and *lesbian* tends to build bridges in my relationships with persons.

We witness to the love of Christ and our care for each other by the terms we use. This partial list is formed out of my own painful experience within the church, an experience that had led to a lot of growth, both personally and in terms of my relationships. But it is also an experience that has distanced some people from me. There are those who choose to turn away, to misunderstand, to condemn. I feel the pain of that separation and/or rejection, but I know that each of us has to make decisions based on our own misunderstandings and readiness. I hope to contribute to growth and community more than to misunderstanding and pain.

In my reading the past years I have become increasingly aware that some of the deepest components in both sexuality and spirituality are similar. I am becoming increasingly fascinated and enriched as I explore that relationship. For example, intimacy, loneliness, faithfulness, and commitment are central in both spirituality and sexuality. They are ways we talk about mystery and relationship that are deeply rooted in the core of our being. We are whole persons, not a conglomeration of sexuality, spirituality, and whatever other categories we construct.

When I read in Henri Nouwen or Thomas Merton about spiritual searching or in Catherine de Hueck Doherty about solitude and the poustiniki, I see the same words and struggles as when I read in James Nelson about intimacy and community. The concern for loneliness and solitude, for love and empathy, for compassion and moral/ethical expression is prominent in each. My ability to live with myself, to know myself, and to commit myself to God and to other persons is basic to both my sexuality and my spirituality. I find that both exciting and scary.

Might it be that I can develop in my spirituality (my discipleship, my Christlikeness, stated in terms of faith) to the degree that I am willing to grow in my sexuality (awareness and acceptance of myself as a complex of passion and need and fear and care)? I experience the two areas to be increasingly parallel.

There are so many areas for further enrichment when we move forward in faith. As I see the suffering in my closeted brothers and sisters, as well as in myself and the world around me, I become impatient to get on with the work of reconciling the world to God and to each other. In education, in witnessing and congregational life, in ministry and mission we have further work to do as a church in responding to the call of the Spirit to be bringers of healing and light. As God's people, called to be the church, we are challenged to come out of our closets of fear and shame, to be more people of compassion and forgiveness.

Keith Schrag is pastor of Ames Mennonite Fellowship in Ames, Iowa.

Chapter 8

PARENTING PARENTS

by Rose Barg

I was 8½ months pregnant with my second child when I found out that Dad had cancer again. Again, because two years earlier he had had to undergo cobalt treatment for cancer of the sinus. Although it was awful and it really aged him, it had been arrested and he had recovered. I sometimes thought it hadn't been so bad after all, because it made Dad realize there were many things he and Mom still wanted to do. They built a new house, reorganized the management of the farm, went on a trip, and generally seemed to be much closer to one another than they had been.

The diagnosis was secondary cancer of the liver. The words seemed deadly. To me cancer had always been one of those catastrophes other people faced, but would never touch my own family.

On top of this, Mom was worse again. She had had rheumatic fever in her youth which left her heart weak due to a damaged valve. We had always known as children that Mom needed a lot of rest, and as well as children could, we had let her have a nap every day. Suddenly, it was time to replace the damaged heart valve without delay.

In early December both Mom and Dad were admitted to the St. Boniface Hospital, Mom for open-heart surgery and Dad for tests and radiotherapy. My daily trek to the hospital began. I had to make baby-sitting arrangements for my three-year-old daughter, since my husband's job kept him out of town for extended periods. I would drop off my little girl, go see Dad on the fifth floor for half an hour, then visit Mom on the fourth. Mom was too weak to get out of bed.

Occasionally, if Dad was strong enough we would help him into a wheelchair and wheel him to Mom's room, so they could be together for a few minutes.

Visiting sick parents took on a routine of its own. My "normal" life became distant and hazy: I left housework undone, rarely saw friends, and could hardly find time to cook a meal or even buy groceries. I was fortunate to have a very sociable daughter, who didn't seem to mind being taken from one relative's house to another or staying with friends long after her normal bedtime, while I was at the hospital.

On one of these hospital visits my ever-thoughtful mother reminded me that the baby was nearly due now. She suggested I carry a bag with me in case I went into labor while I was visiting the hospital. This is exactly what did happen. I went into labor, left the St. Boniface Hospital, picked up my daughter at one place and dropped her off at another, and drove to the Women's Pavilion across town to have my baby. Labor was long and painful, but I remember it was also a relief. All the anguish from the previous days disappeared as I concentrated on my breathing patterns and the regularity of the contractions. And so our little son was born.

I began sending messages to my parents with mutual friends and relatives. I felt very guilty, enjoying my baby and resting in the hospital while they were suffering intensely. I was also angry. Neither of them had responded to their grandchild's birth, there had been no message of congratulation or even acknowledgment of my son's existence. They didn't seem to care. But then I felt guilty again. How could I be so selfish? To need their response and acknowledgment when they were both in such agony?

A chaplain who came to see me helped me sort out these feelings. He pointed out that my baby needed me more at this point than my parents. After all they had an excellent medical staff to look after them, and there were three other siblings who visited them regularly. (Because they all had other full-time commitments elsewhere as well, I suppose I felt most responsible for my parents at this time.) My baby and I, on the other hand, were just beginning to get acquainted in a new relationship that would last all our lives.

Mother's open-heart surgery took place while I was at the Women's Pavilion. My brother and two sisters attended a class at the St. Boniface Hospital to prepare them for this event. Perhaps I was lucky to be in the hospital, because even with all this preparation, one of my sisters fainted when she went to see Mom on the first day. Mom was cold and white; her eyes were bulging and her cheeks sunken; under the various tubes and monitors attached to her she appeared more dead than alive.

I went to see Mom the day I brought my son home. She was already gaining a little strength, although she remained in intensive care for several days.

Dad was released for Christmas, while Mom stayed in the hospital. On Christmas day, we spent the afternoon with her. It was very special. The children were allowed to come in with us. We took Mom to the little chapel downstairs for a Christmas service and communion. Although the service was held by a Protestant minister, it took place in a Catholic chapel, complete with candles, crucifixes, and sisters in habit. That was quite a unique experience for Mom who had always worshiped in a small, rural Mennonite church. But that day was very meaningful to us, and we thanked God that we could celebrate together at such an occasion.

In the middle of January when Mom went home, we finally celebrated a family Christmas. Mom and Dad were both very weak, so we spent most of the day trying to keep the kids quiet so our parents could get some rest.

Mom and Dad made a little agreement to cope with their new life together. They would both look after their own physical needs, and try not to make demands on each other. They were beginning to manage quite well when it became evident that Dad was getting worse again. This time he became resentful. He had always been the strong one, the protector and provider. Once I remember him saying, "You've only had heart surgery. You're going to get better again. But what about me?"

Back in the hospital again, Dad's diagnosis was multiple myeloma, cancer of the liver and the lungs. He received chemotherapy and radiotherapy alternately. He grew very weak, and aged drastically.

Sometimes it was hard to recognize him from one day to the next. One day I walked right by his room and inquired at the nursing station for him. He hadn't been moved, but his hair had fallen out and his teeth were loose. He looked grotesque! I couldn't bear to look at him. I sat beside him on the bed so that I could avoid his face. I showed him photographs of the children and talked nervously and continuously, trying to come to terms with this man who was my dad. I cannot imagine what he was thinking and feeling at this time. I know he didn't want to die. He had many plans that were incomplete. He was at peace with God, but so much of his life was unfinished.

By April he had sunk into a deep depression, physically and mentally. The treatment had been too much for him. He was put in isolation in a dark room. He listened to what was said to him but rarely responded. Once he said, "I would rather be in heaven than suffer like this." He had to be spoon-fed and cared for like a baby, a very frustrating condition for this man who had never been sick in his life and had always prided himself on his youthful agility and independence. The drugs seemed to be affecting his personality; we didn't know how to respond to this person who was listless and cantankerous by turns. We asked for a conference with his doctor. This was most frustrating as well: his heart and his physical condition were still very strong, we were told; a person in Dad's condition could live normally for several years. "Normally," we thought, "O God help us! We can't live like this for several years!"

Dad did begin to improve. He showed an interest in the farm again. He talked about "someday," when he would be better. I realized that he had been aware of our presence and conversation throughout his semiconscious state. He knew that we had expected him to die, and he resented this.

It was very difficult to cope with his "recuperation." It would have been easier for me, emotionally and mentally, if he had died, because I felt that I had been strained to my limit, and so had the rest of the family. We were all exhausted. How long this time? How much longer could we survive with this kind of routine?

In June, Dad was released from the hospital. I went along to stay with him and Mom, since he needed a lot of care which Mom was not strong enough to give. After the first day I realized that I couldn't stay there unless my children were with me. They were so refreshing among all this sickness that even the added strain of looking after them was a welcome relief. I cooked and cleaned. I helped Dad dress and undress. I washed him and took him to the bathroom. He was very embarrassed by this. It had been hard enough to accept help with all this at the hospital, but to expose his weakness to a daughter was very humiliating.

After several weeks, a reasonable routine was established and Mom seemed to be able to handle most of the daily chores with the help of friends and relatives who lived nearby, so I went home with my children. Before a month had gone by, my baby started bleeding rectally. He was admitted immediately to the Children's Hospital for emergency surgery on a congenital ulcer. His blood count was dangerously low. My husband was out of town, everyone was busy with their own problems. I felt my world would end.

My little son. I didn't even know him yet. He was only six months old, and I had spent those six months looking after him mechanically while all my emotional energy had been spent on my parents. I was overwhelmed with a new sense of guilt and neglect.

The baby was in the hospital for two weeks; the ulcer was corrected with major surgery. In those two weeks I was very confused. Could a loving God really do this to me? First Mom and Dad were sick. I had accepted that. They were older, and if they died, at least they had lived a full life. But how could God do this to my baby? Life wasn't making any sense. Sometimes I wished I could just turn off. I was tired of all the responsibility and emotional stress. I wanted to be a kid again! to be taken care of by others; or maybe die. . .

With time, my son recovered, Mom regained strength, and Dad was stable. The family continued to cope. The farm had to be looked after. The harvesting had to be done. Dad tried to supervise from his elevated hospital bed in the living room. He still wanted to be in charge, and my brother, who was doing the actual farm work, complied with his wishes as best he could.

In October, Dad got worse again. This time the medical prognosis was terminal, there was no point in continuing treatments, so Dad was admitted to the local hospital, where Mom could be near him. I went to see him as often as I could, making the eighty-mile trip after work, or staying the weekend. The first few days he responded to our conversations. He would ask how the car was working or who drove today? Where were the children? But soon he lapsed into a semiconscious state, which lasted for twelve days. Sometimes he made motions that he wanted water, or that the lights were too bright, but generally he just lay there.

Out of nowhere, it seemed, we received a new sense of strength and courage. With the help of many relatives, we began a twenty-four hour watch at Dad's bedside. He seemed to appreciate our presence. Each of us would stay with him for a three-hour shift, trying to fit this around jobs, families, and other responsibilities.

Finally the day came when I was called at work to come quickly. I picked up my sister and her baby and drove to the hospital two hours away, wondering if we could make it on time, half hoping that it would all be over when we got there. But Dad was breathing strongly. We could no longer stand the three-hour shifts, so we took turns staying with him for thirty minutes or so. Later in the day we began to stay with him in groups of two or three at a time. We just sat there. We hardly talked, and we could not concentrate enough to read magazines.

We were sure that he would die soon but his heart was still beating strongly. "O God," I prayed silently, "what is the purpose of all this waiting? Hasn't he suffered enough? Why does his heart continue to beat so strongly?"

Around midnight, Dad started to lose his body fluids. There was a terrible smell in the room, the smell of death. We could hardly stand it. But we continued to sit there and watch him, occasionally stroking his forehead (the only place where his skin was not too brittle to touch). Sometimes we thought he responded to our touch, to our words, with a slight flicker of his half-open unseeing eyes. Once, when my sister's husband hummed the melody of an old familiar hymn, we thought we saw tears in his eyes. Was he still aware of us? Could he still hear us?

The night seemed endless. The nursing staff changed shifts; the doctor came in and found his heart still beating strongly. Finally most of the family left to get a few hours of sleep. My brother-in-law, my husband, and I stayed in the room. Dad was breathing less harshly now, but his face was distorted from months of severe pain. His eyes continued to stare, unseeing, through half-open lids.

After two o'clock in the morning, while my husband was holding his hand, my dad skipped a breath, then another, and very quietly stopped breathing altogether. We weren't sure we should believe it. We called the nurse, then Mom and the other family members. They all got out of bed and came to the hospital once more. We stood around the bed of the silent body that had been our dad. The doctor came in and confirmed his death. It was very hard to believe that it was finally over.

We walked over to the waiting room. For several hours we sat there. Months of pent-up emotions began to find release, and we started to laugh and joke around. We laughed about nothing at all. If anyone had seen us they would have thought us a little crazy, giggling in the waiting room at four in the morning. We were not irreverent, but our long year of grieving was over, and we needed relief.

There was a lot of work left to do. We had to plan the funeral, attend to legal matters, and begin to live our own lives again. Mom badly needed a rest. It was less than a year since her heart surgery, and she was still physically weak, although emotionally she had been very strong. There were the children to comfort, and our own feelings to sort out. It would take months before we could recall the dad we had known as a strong, vigorous man.

"Dear God," I prayed as I tried to fall asleep, "thank you for taking Dad. He needed this release from life and relief from pain. Death was the only way to cure all his hurting. He wanted to die now, and we couldn't look after him anymore. His death has lifted a tremendous load from our family. Thank you for being near us during his illness, and thank you for carrying us through, when we felt we couldn't go on. But we still need more help. Continue to look after us in the days to come when Dad's absence becomes a reality. We need your help. Amen."

Rose Barg lives in Pickering, Ontario. She is the mother of three young children.

Chapter 9
life after divorce

by Phyllis Vialoux

I grew up in a Mennonite missionary family in northern Manitoba. I went to school with native children, many of whom came from "broken" homes, with unmarried mothers and other adults in common-law relationships. I was brought up to pity children in these situations. They belonged to people who "didn't know any better"; broken homes were after all the plight of "heathen." These families were often the poorest and most needy in the community. To my mother, I am sure, it would have been an unthinkable catastrophe to consider such a fate for one of her own children. When my brother and his wife's marriage collapsed some thirteen years ago, her embarrassment and shame were very painful and real. Her feelings about divorce have, I think, modified over the years: she is more inclined to sober realism and less to shock and guilt.

The first weeks and months after I left my husband three years ago were filled with anguish, fear, guilt, isolation, relief, and a sense of failure. My whole life had changed. Everything looked and felt different. Often there was a feeling of numbness. I felt tremendous anxiety for my two young children, about the effect of taking them from their home, for the responsibility of raising them alone. I was afraid of the city, having never lived in one except as a student in boarding school. I had no place to live, no job, and no friends except my parents and a few relatives. My youngest child was under a year old, my oldest just four.

It was painful to hear my daughter talk about her father and our old home and friends, all those lost hopes and the dead past. I felt terribly isolated. There was no one to talk to who understood or cared about me personally. I was filled with a sense of failure. My total inability to resolve or "patch up" or change the direction of my marriage, no matter how hard I tried, overwhelmed me: I had failed in this relationship even though there had been moments of love and sharing in it right to the end.

Free moments were islands of nothingness. I remember going home alone after a gathering, standing alone at a bus stop, having no money, no transportation, no furniture—and no importance. My helplessness was embarrassing and hateful to me. Besides trying to cope with my emotions there was the worry of bills, job hunting, court settlements, and lawyers' fees. Totally unloved and drowning in problems—that is how I remember feeling.

There was also relief. I had made a decision, and the depression of a broken relationship and the futility of the future were gone. I had acknowledged openly to myself an insurmountable problem and was finally free. Instead there were thousands of smaller pressures, but I had regained direction and purpose. The future existed again.

The biggest pressures centered around my children. How could I fulfill their thousands of needs when I had so many unmet needs of my own? After an exhausting day at work it is draining to pick up two children and get them to bed, all the while thinking about having to be back at work at 7 a.m.

For me that first year was a test of survival, both financially and emotionally. I obtained a job as a counselor at a juvenile detention center. My mother and father helped out in many ways, and without them and a few other relatives I would not have made it. By the end of the year I had managed to buy a secondhand car and slowly things began to stabilize.

I began attending a Mennonite church. Having been away from the Mennonite milieu for several years, I was amazed at the calm, introspective and "clique-ish" atmosphere I found there. People seemed so "out of touch" with the reality I had experienced. Their problems sounded so minute or else so theoretical. I didn't experience a lot of community in

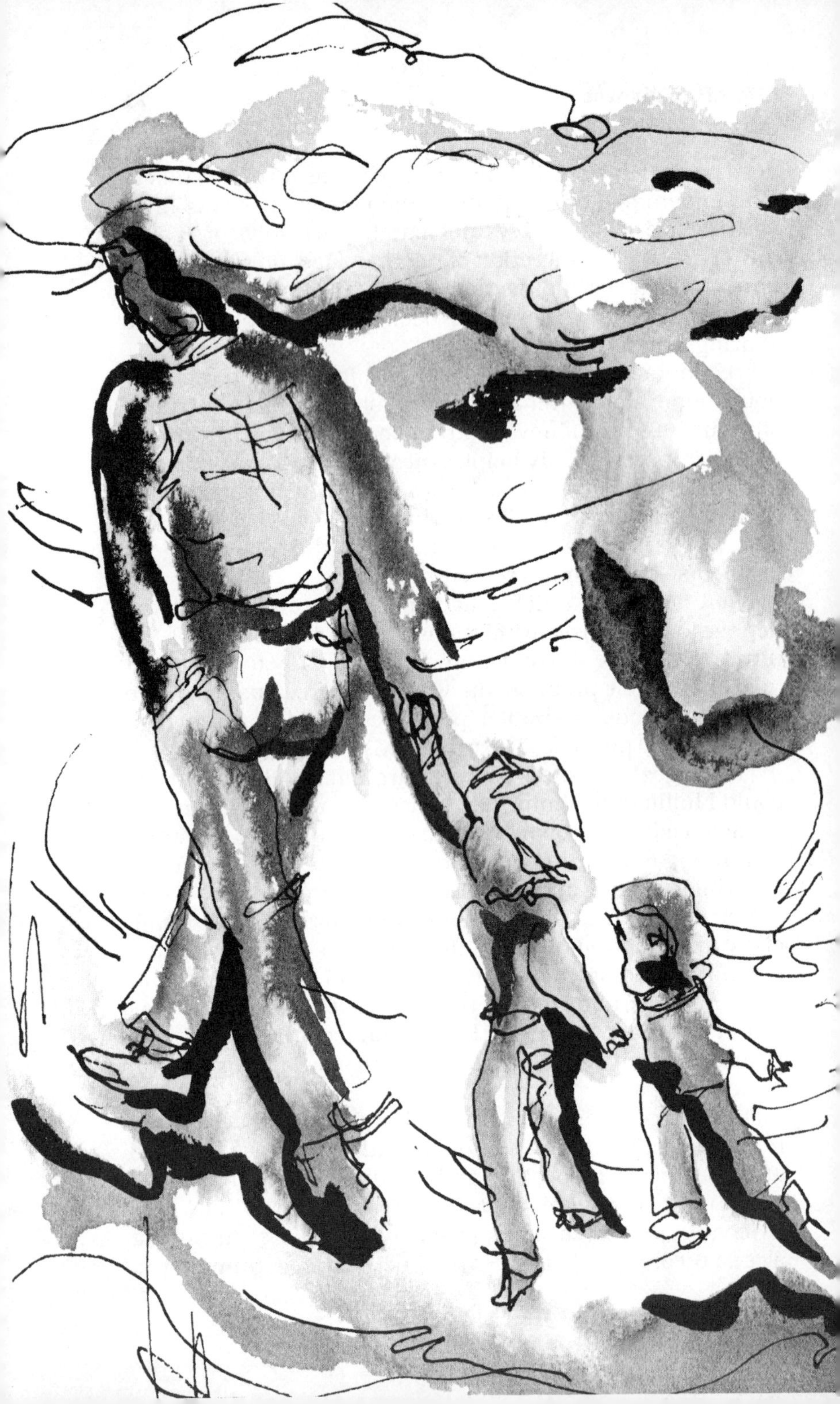

Life After Divorce

the church, but I did have a chance to think through various sermons and other people's opinions. Someone's Uncle John couldn't come for *Faspa* because the weather had cleared and he wanted to combine: this came to me as from another world, another time frame.

My children's day-care providers attended this church and were helpful in making day-care available to me at irregular hours. My mother often looked after the children during Sunday morning services so I could listen to the sermon. These things filled a real need in my life and will always be appreciated.

Many couples found it hard to make conversation with a divorced woman. I found it equally hard to respond to them since I knew most of them had no understanding whatsoever of the turmoil of my experience. People who had themselves been through separation and divorce could be spotted a mile away. They understood. Sometimes I did try to talk to people and was met with incredulous stares, as if to say, "What planet are you from?"

Someone asked me one day, "What would you do if you could do anything you liked for one whole day?" After a moment's thought I knew I would cry all day, preferably curled up with someone who understood. Only I always felt afraid that once I started I would never stop.

One church discussion centered on whether it was Christian to get a divorce, and whether a Christian ought to develop other relationships after divorce. My own personal reaction to these questions was surprise and pain. Surely all persons need meaningful and loving relationships to make life worthwhile; if this possibility is denied to a divorced Christian, then this faith is cruel, unloving, and unjust. It is difficult to give love or be loving if one is not receiving love or being loved. To argue whether divorce is sin seemed to me above all silly. Of course the hardening and "unforgivingness" and selfishness in a marriage that results in a progressively widening communication gap is wrong and "un-Christian" by its very pattern. The results are devastating. However, this does happen to human relationships and separation may become the better alternative or even the only solution to an otherwise destructive situation.

Divorce in my case was not something that happened suddenly. Pressures accumulated through personality and communication blocks over the five years of our marriage. Leaving was the only way finally to save my self-respect and protect my children. I do not feel that leaving my husband was a sin. I do not feel particularly comfortable in a single role. It is not a case of "doing my own thing." It is not possible to take divorce lightly. I would have much preferred to avoid its wounds and its destructiveness.

Single parents especially need a great amount of understanding and support. The struggle to maintain a home and support a family is hard enough for a dual-parent team but this struggle is doubled if not tripled in difficulty for a single parent. How did I ever get into this mess? Will I make it to tomorrow? What did I do to deserve this? Why me? I often found myself asking.

I have learned a lot about myself and about life through the experience of separation and divorce. With God's love and forgiveness, many deep emotional wounds are healing. They leave scars—nothing will ever be the same—but at least life is once again very much worth living. At times I feel as if my chin is just above water in the survival test of life. I suppose this is called coping. I realize that I have gained invaluable insights, and acquired new depth in my value system. A lot of personal ambivalence has been resolved and clarified, both spiritually and emotionally. It is not a route I would recommend to others—but it is my experience and my life.

Phyllis Vialoux works as a counselor at the Manitoba Youth Centre, Winnipeg, Manitoba.

Chapter 10
Losing a Mate

by Elfrieda Tiessen

Outside, the wind was howling around the corner of the house. Earlier in the day, snow had begun to fall and now the wind was blowing it into a screaming blizzard. I had been sitting beside the phone all evening, waiting for the doctor to call. Except for the storm outside, the only sound was the ticking of the clock. I glanced up and saw it was almost ten. Should I call the hospital? No, the doctor said he would call just as soon as there was anything to report.

    The doorbell rang. The sound was so loud - it jarred my whole being! I opened the door and a cold gust of wind fairly pushed the doctor in. "We finished a few minutes ago," he quietly announced. His shoulders drooped with weariness. "Is it bad?" I asked. He nodded and stated simply, "Very bad." I stood there looking at him, my mind a complete blank. I forgot all the questions I had. Dr. Eden pointed to the rocker and said, "Will you sit down?" I watched him slump into the chair opposite me. He shook his head as he rubbed his forehead. "We never expected to find what we did." He paused for a moment, "Jake and I are the same age." He sat up a little straighter and proceeded to give me all the details. My husband would be under heavy sedation at least until morning. As a doctor and good friend he recommended I get a good sleep. "You'll need all your strength in the coming days. Cancer is a cruel disease."

    After Dr. Eden left, I lost all sense of time. The wind had died down. The ticking of the clock was the only sound to interrupt the silence. My youngest daughter Janet (13) was asleep, Kevin (20) was downstairs in the family room. An eternity seemed to have passed since the evening before. Had it only been a little more than twenty-four hours since this nightmare began?

I recalled the events leading up to this evening. Jake walked in from work much earlier than usual and my surprise was cut short by his appearance. He looked tired and his face was ashen. His usually tall body was stooped and he complained of abdominal pains. I suggested calling the doctor but he refused. His work load was heavy. Perhaps all he needed was a good rest. After a long sleepless night of tossing and turning, I suspected Jake's discomfort was more serious than either of us realized. The doctor responded quickly to my call and after a preliminary examination in the emergency room, Jake was admitted to the hospital. The consulting specialist insisted I go home. There would be further examinations and ongoing tests. Dr. Jacobs assured me I would be notified as soon as any results could be determined. True to his word, he kept me informed throughout the day. When the news came that emergency surgery was indicated, I told Dr. Jacobs I would drive to the hospital. He urged me not to. "Stay home with your children, they need you at home," he said. "I'll call you right after we finish in surgery."

The day's events poured through my mind. I was startled when my son came into the room. He sat down on the couch and I gave him the news. After some discussion we decided to wait till morning before calling Pam (18) who was serving a Voluntary Service term in Ohio. And so began the more than two years of heartache, grief, and pain.

My trip to the hospital the next morning was one I will not soon forget. Dr. Eden warned me that Jake was not aware of the seriousness of his condition, neither did he know a colostomy had been performed. I climbed the hospital steps without any idea of what I was going to say or what Jake's reaction would be. Glancing at the clock as the elevator door opened on the surgical floor, I saw it was 8:00 a.m. and the staff was bustling around preparing for doctors' rounds. I slowly walked into the room and stood beside Jake's bed. He opened his eyes and in a groggy voice said, "I'm all tubes." I asked if he was in pain and he answered, "No, just sleepy." He drifted in and out of sleep during the next hour and did not ask any questions. I was grateful because I had no answers.

Dr. Eden suggested I come directly to his office after visiting Jake so that we could decide just how much he should be told. He ushered me into his office and his first question was, "How are you? Did you get any sleep?" This stands out vividly in my mind as it was a long time before anyone else would ask how I was. After some discussion and consultation with the surgeon, we agreed to wait a few days to allow Jake to regain some of his strength before telling him everything. It was obvious I could not tell our friends who might inadvertently say something to Jake during a visit. I made a point of telling our families how important it was to keep this information confidential until Jake had been told. It became increasingly difficult to maintain a cheerful attitude when I visited the hospital. It was almost as though Jake did not wish to hear any answers.

More and more people asked about the nature of Jake's condition. I could only say that the surgery had been for a bowel obstruction. One day I was shocked to get a phone call from one of the women at church. She extended her sympathies and informed me the Bible Study Group was praying that Jake's cancer be healed. I was stunned when she told me a family member had announced to the group what Jake's condition was and that it was terminal. At first I was angry and then frightened. I did not know what this news would do to my husband should he hear it from someone other than the doctor or myself. Dr. Eden was furious. He felt Jake was not ready to hear, but in view of what had occured, he would need to be told immediately. When I got to the hospital later that day, Jake was quiet and quite restless. When I tried to discuss his condition he changed the subject. He did mention "this thing I have," but cancer was not voiced even though I knew he had been told.

Arrangements were made for Jake to go to the Princess Margaret Hospital in Toronto for further consultation and possible treatment. One of the specialists called me into his office and after discussing his diagnosis I asked the question I had not dared to before: "How long?" He looked at me for a moment before replying, "Not long." I felt numb but continued, "How long is 'not long'?" He paused again before he answered, "Maybe three months."

I thought the eighty-mile drive back from Toronto would never end. Jake talked as though he had undergone a simple appendectomy! He told me he was going to build a garage. It would be large enough to hold the family car and his work van, as well as an area for his workshop. I wanted to shake him and ask if he had not heard what the doctors told him just an hour before, but all I could do was sit in stunned silence and listen to all his building plans. We finally arrived home, and after dropping me off he went back to work.

I could not believe what was happening. That evening Jake told friends he was getting better and that he would need to go to Toronto for some tests and treatments but it wasn't anything serious. I was confused and began to wonder if I was the one who did not understand what was happening! Our daughter Pam came home for a brief visit from Ohio and we discussed what was going on. She was bewildered by my information and her father's attitude. Small wonder!

Four weeks later just after Christmas, Jake began chemo and cobalt treatments. After shrinking the tumor they were able to remove it two months later. The hospital staff was amazed at my husband's stamina and quick recovery. After one month they were able to reverse the colostomy as well. No trace of cancer could be detected, but I was warned that should one seedlet have been missed, the cancer would return.

Our lives took on some semblance of normalcy. The three-month period had passed and it was apparent the cancer had lapsed into remission. Our circle of friends was great for socializing and we joined in as much as ever. Jake seemed to be regaining his previous good health and his skin had the look of a healthy tan (in reaction to his treatments). He had put on some weight and looked more like his old self. He was looking so well, I was accused of exaggerating his condition to the point of "burying him before he was dead." This hurt me deeply and has left some painful scars.

Several months went by and Jake went ahead with plans for the garage. He was a builder by trade and when he agreed to hire a contractor to do the actual job, I knew my suspicions were not unfounded. He did not feel nearly as well as he indicated to people. I began to notice other signs but kept my own counsel. It was around that time I developed severe migraine attacks. Jake could not understand these attacks and maintained his own attitude of "if you don't talk about it, it will go away."

My employer and Dr. Eden seemed to be the only ones I could confide in, and to whom I could voice my fears. When I asked Dr. Eden if I was imagining things that were not there as some friends had implied, he replied, "No, you are not imagining anything. Don't hold your breath. The cancer will be back."

My migraines kept getting worse and medication had to be increased. I was sent to a neurologist and underwent a brain scan, electroencephalogram, blood tests, X rays, etc. etc. All the tests came back negative. After a period of thorough questioning he leaned back in his chair and looked at me for a few moments. Then in an almost angry voice he said, "With all that has been going on in your family, you ask me why you have headaches, what the hell do you expect?" He broke his pencil in two and with a few more choice words, dismissed me.

I still had my headaches, but with the assurance there was nothing wrong physically, I carried on. Jake was working very hard. He seemed to be driving himself almost to the point of collapse. He could not say no to any social invitation, so my headaches served a purpose. He would often thank me for turning down another invitation. I was told if we would go out more, my headaches would disappear, that I should stop feeling sorry for myself! I began to feel resentful. Why couldn't we tell our friends he did not feel up to going out? Jake still kept up a good front. When anyone asked how he was, he always replied, "Great!" Others did not see him dragging himself into the house after work; they did not see him push his food away because he could not eat; they did not hear him moan in his sleep.

My husband was dying! I knew it, the doctors knew it, and I was supposed to work from nine to five every day, go on trips, go to parties, go visiting, and have more faith—"Oh God, help me!"

Friends invited us to join them on a two-week trip to Florida. Jake wanted to go and since we both needed the rest, I agreed. Unfortunately, they were not restful days. He couldn't eat, he was in constant pain, and his sleep was restless. I just prayed we would get home before he would need to be hospitalized again.

Four days after we got back to Niagara we were on our way to the Princess Margaret Hospital in Toronto. Yes, the cancer was back. Over a year had passed since that first bombshell had exploded in our lives. To my knowledge, Jake had never voiced the word *cancer*, nor openly acknowledged that he had it. Neither of us spoke for some time as we left Toronto. I was filled with despair until Jake suddenly sat up straight and said, "Now that the cancer is back, we have to make some plans." I sat in stunned silence as he made mental notes about "putting his house in order." I knew then he had known all along but had not been able to share it, even with me. While this hurt, I felt as though a tremendous load had been lifted. Finally, we could talk about his condition!

For the next eight or nine months Jake went to the hospital every Friday morning for chemo treatments besides working every day. My job at the pharmacy was a blessing. My employer and the rest of the staff were understanding and a source of constant strength for me.

When cancer became a part of our lives it seemed to be happening to different people. One of me was going through all the motions that go on when illness strikes, the other me was watching from the outside. One of me was thanking friends for their concern; the other, wanting to cry out, "Why don't you come and pray *with* us instead of just *for* us?"

"Oh God, help me to accept all these cancer cures as gestures of love and concern from well-meaning friends." I was

Losing a Mate

saddened by the annoyance of an acquaintance, when we refused to see a certain faith healer.

"Oh God, I've claimed your promise, I have given you my cares, my worries. Don't let me be tempted to carry them myself."

I lost count of how many persons asked, "How is your husband?" If I told them the truth as the doctors saw it, I was admonished to have more faith.

"Oh God, I've asked you to use the doctors as your instruments, help me to rely on the knowledge and talents you have entrusted them with. Forgive me when I doubt their abilities."

People kept saying, "We've been meaning to come and see you, but it's been so busy."

"Oh, God, help them to realize how much I need those visits, help me to understand that their discomfort of not knowing what to say creates all those excuses for not coming."

Our twenty-fifth wedding anniversary was suddenly upon us. I had neither the strength nor the inclination to organize a formal celebration, so after some pressure from family and friends, we compromised and had an open house. Early in the evening the florist arrived and brought in two beautiful arrangements. When I thanked her she said, "Oh, that's not all!" Before she left she brought in a total of fifteen different plants and arrangements. We were overwhelmed. But for a brief moment, I thought our living room looked like a funeral parlor. Over a hundred friends and neighbors came to wish us well that evening.

Two weeks later Jake again had an attack of severe pain, and after emergency treatment, he was admitted to the local hospital where he was to remain until he died 2½ months later.

My children were a continuous source of support and encouragement to me. Our daughter Pam had cut her Voluntary Service term short and came home several months early. I marveled how God directed us to grow and to trust in him. The hospital staff was most considerate. Since Jake had been coming here during his months of treatment and I had been a patient several times as well, we knew most of the staff personally and they treated us as family. My children and I had visiting privileges around the clock.

A few weeks before Christmas I noticed a lump in my breast. I was too weary to be overly concerned but Dr. Eden moved swiftly, and before I had time to give much thought to myself, I was booked for surgery. Jake was at one end of the hall—I at the other. Since mine was a minor surgery and of a benign nature, I should have gone home the same day, but Dr. Eden was perceptive as well as kind. He kept me in for three days, and since few people knew I was in as a patient, I rested.

At Christmas it was the custom of the hospital to allow the spouse to have Christmas dinner with the patient. The staff invited me to bring my children as well. When we arrived, the nurses had set up a table with white tablecloth, flowers and candles in Jake's room. They brought in a tree and we were asked to sit down. Six nurses served us our turkey dinner. Although Jake had not been able to eat anything for over a month, they brought him a tray as well. I shall never forget that last family dinner! We laughed and joked and occasionally Jake's keen sense of humor came to the surface and we had a relaxed time of fellowship together. Jake was very tired and fell asleep before we left. I returned a few hours later and the first thing he said was, "That was really great! It was as though I had already gone to heaven and watched my family below, everyone enjoying themselves."

Jake's deterioration seemed to be taking place before our eyes. He could not keep any food down, but he never complained. The nurses were kind and did everything they could to make him comfortable. They frequently brought me a cup of tea or asked me to join them for a snack. I learned to love them all.

Few visitors came to the house, and while I was often too tired to notice, it was a lonely existence. This experience has made me intensely aware of how important it is to help families of terminal patients. When a patient can't sleep, they give him or her a pill; when in pain, an injection; when restless, straighten the sheets or give a back-rub. The fam-

Losing a Mate

ily? They go home often to unmade beds, uncooked meals, and usually an empty house. They hurt and spend sleepless nights wondering what the next day may bring.

The last two weeks of his life, Jake was very conscious of the time and often would ask me to stay for "one more hour, maybe then I'll be gone." Then he would send me home and tell me he'd be there the next day. The last evening when I asked if he'd be there in the morning, he said, "I don't think so." At 3:30 a.m. the phone rang. I asked, "Is it over?" The nurse said, "No, but we expect it will be soon." As we walked into the hospital room Janet called, "Dad." We watched him take one more quiet breath and it was over.

"Oh God, we asked that you would take him gently, thank you for hearing our prayers."

We went back to our house and I sat down at the kitchen table to make a list of things that I needed to do in the morning. I realized my weariness was all gone, and I was able to carry out all that needed to be done. The next few days are somewhat of a blur.

After the funeral there was not much time to sit around. Jake had insisted Pam and her fiancé not change their wedding plans and so six weeks later they were married. My heart was not really in it and sometimes I wonder if they will ever feel shortchanged, but somehow I believe they understood.

I felt a great need to be able to get away all by myself and prayed for this to happen in some way. But there was so much to be done. Two weeks after the wedding I accepted an invitation to accompany the hand-bell choir (of which Janet was a member) on a Good-Will tour of Haiti. It was a good week for me and I felt refreshed, but unfortunately before we arrived home I began to feel ill and two days later had to be hospitalized with a severe case of Shigela Dysentery. I was to spend the next eleven days in isolation with only an occasional appearance of a nurse or another specialist. The first five days I was too sick to care what happened to me but as I began to feel better, I had my days alone. I thank God for those days. I had a lot of thinking to do.

Before Jake died we discussed our home and other belongings which I would need to take care of. It would be impractical for me to keep the house since I couldn't possibly look after the property. We made a lot of decisions that I would need to carry out. Visitors came infrequently so I had lots of time to look after all the details.

After I had completed the sale of the house, I was suddenly surrounded with concerned people who were shocked at my decisions. I was extremely bitter. Why should anyone care now? Hardly anyone had been near us in weeks to show interest or concern in how we were doing. I wasn't making any rash or sudden decisions. Jake and I had decided all this together months before. Not everyone was insensitive. I am reminded especially of a couple who dropped in one evening and when I mentioned a leak in my sink, the man went outside to get his tools from his van and fixed the problem. One morning a neighbor cleared my driveway before I even realized I would not be able to get out. How I thank God for these and other kind friends!

A few months later the possibility of a job in Winnipeg came to my attention and my children encouraged me to look into it further. As a result, Janet and I moved at the end of August, nearly eight months after Jake's death. The move was not an easy one for me, but with the help of many relatives and new friends, it turned out to be a positive one.

I've questioned and learned much about being a widow. Peculiar attitudes surface about and towards someone who has experienced a loss by death. People attend the funeral and bury both halves of the couple or put the remaining one in a box by avoiding the bereaved. Becoming a widow suddenly made me an incomplete social unit. I am rarely invited to dinner parties. It seems difficult to arrange a table with an odd number. People have often said, "Drop in sometime." But, they seldom say when.

I long sometimes to sit down and just talk to someone—about everything or nothing—but most people are just too busy. I experience loneliness most when I'm in a crowd of people. Do my feelings of depression make me a neurotic as some are prone to imply? Does my loneliness constitute a lack of faith?

It seems mourning is affected by the expectations of society. No tears...something isn't right. Tears...lack of faith. Glib answers from someone who has never experienced death can only bring about resentment. "It's a blessing he/she could go," "God never makes mistakes," or "All things work together for good" often reveal the inadequacy of people coming to terms with their own impending death. The important thing is not to say something, but just to be there to lighten the burden.

I have often found my simplistic faith being tested—and found wanting. God does not fill the void as some well-meaning friends told me. I believe God enables *us* to fill the void as we become ready and able to do this.

My biggest disappointments have come about when I think of myself as a friend of couples and suddenly realize I'm the fifth wheel and am no longer a part of many couple-social patterns. Time *does* heal, but I have experienced that it takes costly expanses of my life with it. The pain of rejection has dulled. The agony of "not fitting in," in situations I formerly took for granted, is not so intense.

Sometimes I find myself exhausted from expending so much energy in an unconscious effort to avoid grieving. At these times, I value the assurance of my Lord who helps me "draw near to the throne of grace, that (I) may receive mercy and find grace to help in time of need" (Heb. 4:16 RSV).

Elfrieda Tiessen coordinates the Resource Centre for the Conference of Mennonites in Canada, Winnipeg, Manitoba.

Chapter 11
SURVIVING SUICIDE

by Gayle Wiebe

It's just a little over a year now since my brother died. He took his own life—he committed suicide. In an instant the memory of that awful day when the police came to our home and told us of finding my brother's body in his car with a hose attached to the exhaust and running into the back window comes rushing back. Often it is unbidden, but sometimes I almost seem to torment myself with the memory. Either way, it is something that will always be with me. The initial shock, the denial of its truth, the retching feeling in the pit of my stomach are all still very real and very close. Tears can come at any moment, often at a word or two spoken on TV or something said in a group that seems unrelated but triggers the memory just the same. Often I wake up on a seemingly ordinary day with a feeling of a weight on my shoulders, a feeling that all is not right. It takes a moment or two and then everything comes flooding back. Of course all is not right—my own brother committed suicide. He no longer wished to live. In fact, he wished to die. Of course everything is not all right!

But all of these reactions, these feelings, go unnoticed by others. I laugh at jokes and humorous situations. I study and I work. I go to school and to church. I go out with friends and enjoy myself. I read and listen to music and I talk. I eat and I drink and I sleep. I live a "normal" life. Friends and acquaintances may consider me a somewhat "moody" or "serious" person but I don't stand out. I don't attract attention. Those who know of the tragedy that befell my brother and my family say I have coped amazingly well. Those who don't know my background would never guess the experience I have had with suicide.

They say I've coped remarkably well. Coped? My initial reaction to that is to say I haven't coped at all. I still mourn and miss my brother. I still cry when I think of the agony and suffering he must have gone through both in fighting for his life and in giving it up. Feelings of anger still come to me and I want to scream, "Why did this have to happen to my brother?" and "Why did it have to happen to me?"

And this is only the tip of the mountain of questions that plague me every day since my brother's death. Different people commit suicide for different reasons. We hear often enough of great movie stars and rich businessmen who commit suicide after broken love affairs or unsuccessful business ventures. We hear of violent deaths and seemingly calm, quiet deaths. Some people who commit suicide leave notes, others don't. Some seem to be saying, "Won't they all be sorry when I'm gone," and others just seem to be unable to handle life anymore. I try so hard to understand why my brother felt it necessary to take his own life. I want to know what he was thinking and feeling. I want to know what his death means.

I knew my brother for twenty years. I lived with him for most of those years, yet it seems as if that young man who bore my brother's name and took his own life a little over a year ago must have been someone else. I just can't really begin to imagine what this person, whom I thought I knew, was really feeling. I can only have a vague idea of the utter torment and despair with life that must lead one to such a final action.

How can one cope with the realization that you never really knew a person you loved? In my mind "cope" means to overcome difficulties or problems. I'm not sure one can "cope" with suicide and its aftereffects. Suicide brings up so many unanswerable questions. So how can one overcome this? I am and think always will be asking questions that don't have answers.

But I keep on living. I haven't died along with my brother. I'm still here stuck with all the problems and questions I had before plus a few more. I also still have the joy that life can bring. I'm "surviving." I think that's a better word than "coping." I have survived the death of my brother, but things will never be as they were before. The picture I have in my head as I think of this is one of a whole person with a piece missing. This is often the way I feel—as if a part of me is gone. That part cannot be replaced. It's gone forever. Neither can it be covered up or ignored. It must be accepted and lived with. Recrimination and embarrassment are futile. Nevertheless, that missing piece strongly affects how the rest of the whole works.

I feel as if the whole world can see my missing piece. People try desperately to ignore it, thinking it is something of a disgrace. You see, nobody wants to talk about suicide very much. It is not a pleasant subject because it makes us think too much, especially about death. For me this leads to a terrible feeling of loneliness. Why as soon as I mention that my brother died or that he took his own life, do people say "oh" and change the subject of the conversation? It helps to talk things out. One needs to verbalize the questioning that any death and especially suicide brings out. If one is not able to do so, the questions become tormenting and the loneliness that one feels is excruciating.

One reason that suicide is a difficult subject to talk about is because of the judgment that always seems to be involved. As a young teenager I remember being faced with a hypothetical suicide situation and being asked whether I thought it was right or wrong. I didn't ponder the question long. I determined that suicide was wrong and probably one of the worst sins at that. After all, the Bible says "Thou shalt not kill," and suicide is murder. And suicide is like telling God, "I want no more to do with your creation, the world." This is what I thought. I had suicide in a nice neat package and safely filed away in my memory as well as my subconscious. This way whenever I was faced with the news of a suicide either on TV or in a book or newspaper I could quickly make a judgment on that person and the terrible thing he or she did.

I don't think I'm the only one who has thought this way

about suicide. For many it seems such a distant reality that it is quite easy to make a judgment on those directly involved. It's the same with many kinds of emotional problems. How often have you heard something like "Well, of course he has problems, just look at his home life!"? This is judgment not only of the person with the problem, but of his or her entire history and all persons involved in that history, especially the family.

This way of thinking does not automatically change when a person in your own family has a problem. With my brother's suicide came judgment. Judgment by others and by myself. I was tormented by the judgment I immediately made on my brother and his act of suicide. What I had always thought in regard to suicide said that my brother had committed an unpardonable sin. Yet it seemed totally unfair because he was not a bad person. He was a Christian. We are assured forgiveness of our other sins. Why is suicide different? Over and over I asked, "Will my brother be able to enter God's heaven?" My teaching told me no and so I had judged my brother. But the judgment seemed so wrong, so along with judgment came guilt.

But I didn't only judge my brother. I judged myself as well. I had always accepted the psychology that said one can find the roots of one's problems in the family. Did this mean that I was a major contributor in some way to my brother's decision to end his life? I believed so. With this judgment came even more guilt. Often when people refused to talk with me about my brother's death or seemed to feel uncomfortable with me because of it I've felt that they were judging me or my brother. They may have been doing nothing of the sort but it still felt like a judgment because I felt so guilty already. All of this combined leads to an overwhelming sense of guilt that is not easy to get rid of. In fact, I didn't want to get rid of that terrible feeling because I believed that I deserved it.

Very slowly I have felt a lessening of that burden of guilt. But it is not gone. I've had to rethink many things that were very much a part of what I believed before. My faith in God has had to be reevaluated. I've had to work through my upbringing that told me that suicide is an unforgivable sin and how this conflicted with the deep conviction I feel that God will have mercy on my brother. His suicide was not an act of contempt for God. My brother found life very painful and I believe that his death was a cry for help and mercy. I cannot believe that God could turn away from such a plea. This doesn't mean that questions don't remain. They do. But I no longer believe that I know how God will judge. No one can know. Judgment must be left to God.

The guilt that I enforce on myself through judgment does not leave me easily, however. The biggest and most difficult question after a suicide must be, "How could I have stopped it?" At least it has been for me. Even now I go through the events of the week or two before my brother died and wonder "If I would have done this or that would it have changed anything?" And with this comes the question, "Why did things happen as they did?" and "Why didn't I do that instead of this?" These questions don't have answers, and that is precisely why they are so painful. Living with unanswered questions is a difficult thing to do. But that is precisely what must be done. I am trying to accept those questions without answers as a part of me and what I believe. I think it is a lot like faith. In fact, for me it has become an expression of my faith. I must accept these questions realizing that I may never know the answers or that there may not even be any answers. Being at peace with this uncertainty is a long and difficult process.

So much has happened to me in the year since my brother's suicide. Sometimes I feel as if I've aged at least twenty years. But in reality, time has gone on as it always has and my brother's death is just another statistic to millions of people. For me it has been like a nightmare. Many times I've thought that sooner or later I'd wake up and find out it all wasn't true. But it *is* true and life goes on.

Have I coped with my brother's suicide? I don't really think so. My brother's death has changed my life. Suddenly my easy life is no longer so easy. What I'd always believed in suddenly doesn't seem so certain. Suddenly I'm filled with guilt and loneliness. Suddenly I've got a thousand questions that don't seem to have answers. How does one overcome these problems? I don't think it's possible. The questions, the guilt, and the loneliness stay with you. That missing piece can never be replaced. This could be unbearable.

Many times I have wondered if I could survive the aftermath of my brother's suicide. Now I believe that I will survive. I'm surviving the guilt and the loneliness. And I'm trying to accept the unanswerable questions that race around in my head. I still come up with new questions that don't seem to have answers. Things don't seem black and white anymore. I'm trying to deal with the fact that there aren't many certainties in life.

I am surviving. But there is no way I could do it on my own. The tightening of my family into a close and warm support group makes a difference. Friends who are willing to talk and listen and cry with me also help to lessen the pain. But most important is the comfort and care that only God can give. Through all the pain, the questioning, and the loneliness, I have felt the unfailing love of God. With God's understanding I am slowly feeling less of a need to understand everything myself. It is not an easy thing—to survive. But I believe in the promise that Peter talks of when he says, "Cast all your anxieties on him, for he cares about you.... And after you have suffered a little while, the God of all grace, who has called you to his eternal glory in Christ, will himself restore, establish, and strengthen you" (I Peter 5:7 and 10 RSV).

Gayle Wiebe is completing her bachelor's degree in Education at the University of Manitoba.

Chapter 12
homosexuality: two perspectives

by Bev Scott and Kris Lane

"I'm a homosexual, Bev." These words fell on ears that could only cope with the superficial. I didn't know how to respond. I wasn't in touch with my feelings about the information that was given to me—after fifteen years of marriage and two children. I was stunned and responded out of the part of me that knows how I "should" react. My feelings were buried deep inside and would only begin to surface three years later. (This process of surfacing is still at work.)

At a rational level, my response was acceptance. I reassured my husband that I loved him, that I appreciated the courage it had taken to tell me. I could relate to the pain he had suffered carrying this secret with him for years, and I appreciated that he loved himself enough, at last, to trust me to hear a secret that would affect both of us. I told him it didn't change my love for him, that all that had really happened was that now I knew more about him than before. We would work through whatever happened—together.

I processed the information and filed it for further reference. I didn't talk to anyone, nor did I give much thought to the subject during those years. Certainly, there were times when my husband and I talked about the situation, but nothing was decided about our future, together or separately. Neither of us wanted to separate. We loved each other. There was no third party, so we decided to stay together and continue our relationship as it had always been.

During a bout of spring housecleaning three years later (a

time of mental housecleaning as well) I was suddenly aware of what my husband had told me. I realized I didn't have a means of supporting myself, never mind my family, if/when the day arrived that my husband said he was leaving. This was the first sign that my information had finally moved from being in intellectual storage to being a fact I could face. It was then that I could feel. It was then that I was able to start reacting to my needs.

Within two weeks, I had made arrangements for taking a course as a secretary, a marketable skill that was portable, always in demand; and although not on my list of things I most wanted to do, would provide the financial means to keep us together as a family. I had moved from denial to a position of activity. It had taken this long for me to subconsciously allow myself to deal with a topic for which I had no guidelines or "shoulds."

Initially I heard the words and lived with them. They were attached to feelings of anxiety, apprehension, guilt, and anger—although the anger has only been allowed in bits and pieces and I'm really only coming to terms with this now. The anxiety and fears were for my future as a single parent and for our children in that setting. There was also considerable fear and anxiety for the future of my husband. (It is a tall order to begin again with a lifestyle that is socially unacceptable after reaching the age of forty.) At this point I tried talking seriously to my husband, but the conversations were filled with "what if's." Even then we were not seriously contemplating a separation. I lived in a fantasy that we could work something out that would be acceptable to us all.

During the summer I watched my husband lose a considerable amount of weight. He looked years older than he was. He wore an expression of sadness and despair. The years of trying to live a life that didn't fit his reality were beginning to take a noticeable toll. I can't imagine what it would be like to live for forty years trying to fit into a lifestyle that didn't work. My husband wanted desperately to be acceptable and fit into society. He tried very hard to deny the feelings within him that didn't coincide with the norms in which he had been raised and believed. He hoped that if he married and raised a family (did all the right things) that these feelings would go away. He felt great guilt and a sense of worthlessness because of the social conditioning against homosexuality and the stigma attached to being a social misfit. There was then the added guilt of having included the kids and me in this "impossible dream." He loved us and didn't want to see us hurt, but it was fast becoming a life and death situation.

I secretly hoped that my going back to work would relieve some of the pressure and perhaps make it possible for us to live our lives in some degree of comfort. *Separation* and *divorce* were words that we avoided. We talked all around what was really concerning both of us and slowly eating us up. We were so afraid of what we instinctively knew was ahead.

After a summer holiday (the best we can remember as a family) we settled back into our routine. One of the real pleasures my husband and I shared was to take long walks in the evening. The evening before school started the children were having difficulty settling down, so I suggested to my husband that he go for a walk without me while I stayed at home with them. The walk became a "cruise" and the turning point of our lives. Within a very short time I was aware that my husband was out more than he was at home. I hung between fear (for his safety) and anger (that he would do this to us). The night before I started back to school (with my anxieties about returning to school, questions about being a good mother when I couldn't be at home for my kids, and excitement about starting a new phase of my own life), my husband arrived home late. When I asked him to fill me in on what had happened, he said he wanted a separation with view to divorce. There! my worst fears were out. The words had been said! Now, what?

My first days back at school were spent in shock. I attended to the obvious. I went to classes, learned the ropes after being away from institutional learning for many years. I prepared meals and did my household chores—all with my mind whirling. How was I going to manage? I'd never been on my own. I had gone from my family home to a university residence to a structured technical training program to my marriage. How would we survive?

In the outside world, I tried to operate as if there was nothing wrong with my life. I tried to keep a semblance of normality for the kids. This was very difficult. We had never been a couple that argued, and now we were fighting every time we were together. The kids were confused and upset. I was extremely upset, and scared beyond belief. My husband (it seemed to me) couldn't wait to get away from the house and family and be with the new person in his life. I was angry, jealous, and feeling rejected. I couldn't talk to anyone for fear of breaking down. I didn't want to hear questions from anyone else because there were so many of my own going unanswered.

Surprisingly, a part of me that knows how to live seemed to take over. The shock of my reality had short-circuited my usual intellectual "rationalizing" and shifted gears for me so that I was operating on instinct. I went to talk to the staff counselor assigned to me. I told her what was happening and that there would likely be days when I would be there in body but not in mind. She was very understanding and supportive. (In fact, there were days when she told me to go home because school wasn't where I should be that day.) I then contacted a friend who had acted as my therapist on previous occasions and arranged to get professional help and support. I realized I didn't want to live with the situation building up inside me without somewhere to go. All this took place in the first three days after my return to school. By the end of the week, I felt that I could make it, somehow. I realized the first week was behind me and I'd survived.

At the beginning of the second week, I went to see my Manpower counselor and told her of my changed status—from supported spouse to single parent/student. Before I knew what had happened she called to say I had been accepted for full benefits. This financial support meant that we could afford an apartment for my husband and our volatile situation would be eased. This news relieved some of the pressure for my husband also. Tight finances were another cause for anxiety between us.

Gradually I began sharing with my friends the events of my life. I couldn't begin to share with more than one or two, initially. I was anxious about telling my family of our pending separation and divorce. "Separation" would be hard to hear—but what would they do with "homosexual"?

At this point in my life I didn't have a church affiliation. My membership in church had long since fallen into a state of perpetual absence. However, during the second week at school, I met a woman with whom I was to discover that I really had a very strong personal faith. She was for me a person who really lived her faith. She was full of joy and laughter. She taught me how to laugh again. She talked of her faith in and around every subject we discussed. I came to realize that I was made of good stuff and could cope quite well, thank you very much.

Added to the positive side of the ledger was a dear friend who had herself recently separated from her husband. Friends for years, we promptly began ministering to one another. We talked about our fears, our anger. We "poor me'd," we cried, we talked frequently and long. The process continued for more than a year until we thoroughly sickened ourselves of the topic. After this we could begin doing things that were fun and reconstructive for ourselves.

This may sound very self-indulgent and no doubt was; but it was what we both needed. We both short-circuited our rational minds and dealt with our innermost feelings—our pain, our loss, our confusion. We shared what it was like to be alone, what it was like to raise our families alone. We discussed how we related to our extended families and their feelings of loss and confusion. We had many mutual concerns.

However, she could not relate to the reasons for my separation any more than I could relate to hers. I longed to talk to someone who had faced this situation. I wanted to find out how they dealt with their feelings, how they told their families, how they supported their children and answered their questions, and how they dealt with the feelings of rejection—of not being good enough. I was sure there were people out there. But where? The sense of being alone was heavy to bear. Feeling "different" didn't help either. I talked with social workers, counselors, clergy—a lot of people I had grown to depend on for help and direction. They all listened sympathetically, but none of them could (or did) say: "Bev, I know some people who have been through this. Would you like to talk to them?"

As I've related my story in abbreviated form, I'm aware of leaving out a lot of events and feelings. I haven't related the story of my children and their struggle, or any of the struggle my husband went through. These feelings are rooted in real needs, too. The everyday chores of living (attending classes, maintaining a household, relating to the outside world) were things attended to as if I were an automatic pilot. The feelings were so painful that we couldn't leave them "on the surface" to be seen by the world. The old habit of "saving face" operates in all of us. The longer we leave these feelings hidden from the world, the easier it becomes to continue avoiding the real issue. As we avoid the feelings with others, we in turn help ourselves to avoid the feelings within ourselves. This doesn't mean they've gone away; it means they are buried. We can bury feelings and avoid dealing with them for varying periods of time, but feelings will eventually have to be faced and dealt with.

As the result of support by caring friends and family, I grew in strength and understanding. I have learned a great deal about homosexuality in the past six years and have, in turn, tried to help others in coming to terms with their learning. To this end, Families of Gays was begun nearly four years ago. This is a support group or system, designed to help family members with their adjustment to the news, "I'm a homosexual."[1]

There are numerous books available in the public library.[2] There are people willing to talk and share their stories and help in the realization that we are not alone. This holds true for the homosexual member of the family as well as for those of us who are straight. In fact, I believe it falls to those of us with a vested interest in both worlds who will have to bridge the gap between the "gays" and "straights." Homosexuals have been "in the closet" but their families are often "in the attic." It is with understanding and a willingness to learn and grow that we will all have our day in the sun.

Bev Scott works as a secretary at St. Boniface Hospital, Winnipeg, Manitoba, and coordinates Families of Gays, a mutual support group.

NOTES

1. Families of Gays offers information and mutual support for spouses, parents, and children of homosexuals. Address is: Families of Gays, Box 1912, Winnipeg, Manitoba, Canada R3C 3R2.
2. For example, Betty Fairchild and Nancy Wayward, *Now That You Know: What Every Parent Should Know About Homosexuality* (New York: Harcourt, Brace and Jovanovich, 1979); and Penelope Russianoff, *Why Do I Think I Am Nothing Without a Man?* (New York: Bantam, 1982).

2.

Growing up in a rural midwest atmosphere in the 1950s and '60s in a multigenerational Mennonite family, provided me with little or no exposure to homosexuality. In fact, most of my time and energy during high school, college and graduate school were devoted to studying and excelling as a student and getting recognition for such. I was known as an easygoing person with casual friends, but unable to develop any close trusting relationships with any of my peers, especially the males. I seldom dated. I fantasized about having close personal friendships with specific jocks in school but never took any action to develop such friendships and when I was approached by them in a friendly way, I would tend to panic and even become physically ill.

Leaving home for college was traumatic in the fact that while I saw becoming a college student, and later a professional social worker, as a way to gain some recognition and learn how to relate to people, I was also threatened by the prospect of leaving my family with the accompanying feelings of loneliness and isolation. With the help of some of my relatives in the college area, I was able to at least tolerate the university setting for the first few weeks and then slowly began to feel comfortable there even though my interests were not the same as my male peers, who were high on dating and macho behavior.

After obtaining my master's degree in social work, I secured a job as a psychiatric social worker and was immediately exposed to patients with various backgrounds and lifestyles. I learned to know the psychiatric staff in this urban hospital and because of their warmth, openness, and interest in me, I began truly to grow personally and become more "feelings" oriented rather than just "intellectually" oriented. Being out of school for the first time in my life, I was no longer able to hide so easily behind my books and since it was necessary for me to assist my patients in dealing with their feelings, I was forced to do the same. I began to realize that I was very lonely, and the small taste of having caring people around me at work whetted my appetite for more, but all renewed attempts at dating were dismal failures and completely unsatisfying. While finding girls to date was no problem, the only enjoyment I received from a date was giving a sigh of relief as I dropped her off at her home. The more I forced myself into these situations, the more I found myself fantasizing about having close buddy friendships with some of my male friends at work and found myself obsessed about them and becoming jealous of their wives or other friends.

This discomfort led me to begin speaking to my feelings—bizarre as they seemed to me at the time—to another male friend whom I had learned to trust, and as our conversation became more intimate, so did our total relationship. Finally this led to my first homosexual experience with this friend at the age of twenty-six. And that was when it seemed as if the world would come to an end! I was suddenly faced with the fact that I was probably gay. No doubt I had been denying it for a number of years, but now I had to face up to this. While on the one hand it was somewhat of a comfort to know that this could have been why it was so difficult for me to develop relationships like other people through the years, I now had to deal with the possibility that I was headed for hell according to my understanding of the Scriptures.

Agitated and depressed by this revelation, I began reading everything I could get my hands on regarding homosexuality and Christianity. I spoke to a couple of elders in my church and wrote to various well-known Mennonite leaders for counsel. One church member was very supportive of me, saying that this was an individual decision that I must make without any dictates from the church. Another person in the church suggested therapy. The most hostile and hurtful response came from my pastor who wanted to bring this matter to the whole congregation and asked me to consider resigning positions as our church council chairman, Sunday school teacher, and mission board member. While initially I considered dropping out of the church, I came to the conclusion that God loved me and since he made me as I was, I must learn to live in an ethical way with my sexuality. I enjoyed my church involvement and would not let anyone deprive me of this. I did choose to go into therapy to help me deal with the ongoing problem of self-acceptance. At no time did I consider myself as "sick" but often as a "sinner."

I am now convinced, however, that I did not choose to be gay and will not choose to be celibate. I will continue to work on developing close, intimate relationships with both males and females, but sexual ones with males only. Therapy also has helped put my sexuality in perspective. There is much more to me than just my sexual behavior, and I must always keep my relationship to Christ as my number one concern. My professional obligations, church, social action, and political activities are all important also. My family also ranks very high on my list of priorities. Unfortunately I feel I can share none of this with them. Their life has not been easy either and while it took me several painful years to accept my homosexuality, I would expect it to be even longer for them. I do not question them about their sexual activities and they do not question me about mine.

Meeting other gay people, especially gay Christians, has been of the utmost importance for me. By becoming active in gay social and political and growth groups and the Metropolitan Community Church, I have gained the support I needed and developed close friendships. By being selective as to which of my heterosexual friends, both in and out of the Mennonite church, I confide in, I have been able to feel accepted and free to be me. It is interesting that three out of the five church council members, who are all professionals and leaders in various ways in our small Mennonite church, are gay. We are closeted in many ways, but slowly becoming more open.

For a long time my hope was to develop a monogamous relationship with another gay male and "live happily ever after." My expectations have changed a bit as I've matured. Considering society's tendency to condemn and ignore the sincerity of these relationships, and my own tendency not to commit myself completely to a relationship without at times having to deny that it exists (such as to my family), I am aware of the odds against such happening. Yet, I'm idealistic enough to hang on to a bit of that hope. For one year, I did live with a young man whom I considered my "partner," but it became obvious that we would both be happier living apart.

I continue to want to share my time, money, interests, and happy and sad times with another male in both an intimate and sexual way and if I do this with someone for only ten years, ten months, or even just ten days, I consider that better than not at all. It is not easy to build a relationship without the benefit of tradition, law, clerical, or congregational support. But I am determined to do that for myself, step by step with much soul searching and consultation and sharing with many others. This is not a simple process but one filled with doubts and fears along the way, yet I can tell you without a doubt that I am happier and more contented in this task than I have ever been before.

Kris Lane is a pseudonym.

Chapter 13
becoming god's people
by Lynne Martin

I sit in a classroom, the only Christian, and listen to my Jewish classmates playing the Mennonite Game:

"Rabbi H---- allows mixed seating in his synagogue."

"His daughter Rachel is my second cousin."

"Really! She's my brother's girl friend's best friend."

"My mother went to school with Mrs. H----."

What began as a potentially theological discussion has turned into genealogical puzzle solving, gaining immediacy for the participants as it does so. Perhaps this is as it should be; after all, Matthew thought such an activity to be so important that his Gospel begins with Jesus' bloodline, though his purpose is clearly theological.

A new student joins the class. He was brought up as a Christian but has converted to Judaism for theological reasons. He sits silently while his adopted brothers and sisters in the faith make relational connections of which he is not a part—even though his conversion took place nine years ago. He resorts to making disparaging remarks about his Christian background in order to "prove" himself, to be one of them. I am embarrassed for him; his frustration has been mine. I, too, have felt the grip of that need to belong which can drive its victim to act contrary to his/her convictions. This is the power behind the dare, the peer pressure from which mature adults are not exempt. It is also the glue that keeps social groups intact and orderly, and which can motivate an individual to adhere to his/her convictions in the face of tremendous adverse pressure. It has been a force both positive and negative in my own search for meaning.

I am Mennonite by choice, not birth. My background is Lutheran with a smattering of Catholicism: How did I come to participate in the Mennonite family/identity?

For me, the need to be one of God's people (1 Peter 2:10) started in childhood. As an adopted child I often felt a sense of alienation. My parents had nothing to do with it; they have always made me feel loved and in a special way, chosen. Perhaps the very fact of being adopted created my feeling of not belonging. Since I attended five different schools from kindergarten through grade six, I had a constant image of myself as the "new kid in town." My family has always been strong on keeping certain holiday rituals, and for this I am deeply grateful, because though I wasn't aware of it then, my interest in religion was closely bound to my need for roots, for a sense of history and continuity. Family rituals helped to fill that need.

My parents' church also did much to satisfy me. I loved participating in the liturgy, which seldom varied, so that I soon could recite most of it by heart. This was *my* church, *my* worshiping act. I could depend on its stability. I belonged to it.

But sometime during my adolescence that stability crumbled. For some reason families began moving out of our congregation, until my brother and I were the only children left. This change was gradual, but I remember feeling bewildered when schoolmates would talk about weekend young people's activities in their various churches. Our congregation didn't have even a youth Sunday school class. (In fact, there was only one adult class, attended by a handful of sweet but elderly women. We had very little to say to one another.)

Meanwhile, every night at eleven o'clock I lay awake listening to the newscasters announcing the numbers of dead Americans in Vietnam. My catechism training had introduced me to the doctrine of Church/State separation, which I understood as rendering unto Caesar those things that are Caesar's and unto God, God's. This meant that obedience to the State was separate from obedience to God, though the two were not mutually exclusive. However, I reasoned, if these allegiances were separate, they could also at times be different; therefore, obedience to God might sometimes require disobedience to the State. Furthermore, I had been taught Jesus' instruction to turn the other cheek, not to mention the commandment, "thou shalt not kill." How could there be such a thing as a "just war"? My congregation wasn't able to help me work through this issue. The library became flat and repetitious for me; the sense of security there seemed more and more like unreal complacency. On the outside I participated as much as ever, but inside I was seething with frustration. I didn't belong in any meaningful way anymore.

When I entered university a few years later, I began attending mass with my Catholic roommate. I had grown up in a Catholic neighborhood and had been intrigued by the sense of solidarity among my Catholic friends. The Lutheranism I knew had nothing overtly identifiable about it, though its ethnic roots were German; and though my maternal grandmother, who lived with us, spoke German occasionally, my family and my congregation were thoroughly Americanized. Furthermore, the idea that I could turn to other Lutherans for personal guidance seemed unthinkable after my experience.

Catholics, on the other hand, seemed somehow set apart. They had a certain vocabulary, a social structure that seemed different from what I thought of as mainstream America. Their houses and cars looked like everyone else's, but inside the houses were rosaries and missals and statues of saints. They wore St. Christopher medals and ate fish on Fridays. They had separate schools run by priests and nuns. They had large extended families living in close proximity. They had leaders like the Berrigan brothers and Mother Teresa. And they seemed to belong to one another in a way that appealed to me.

More important, perhaps, they were my own age. Since there were no young people in my own congregation, I adopted the practices of my neighborhood peers in order to belong to them. (Besides, I was in love with the Catholic boy across the street.) I learned how to cross myself and to genuflect. I learned what a mantilla is and how to say the Hail Mary. It was only natural for me to pursue my interest in Catholicism once I moved out of my parents' home.

Ultimately, theological dissatisfaction led me away from becoming Catholic. I couldn't accept the church hierarchy which implied that some people had more access to God than I did. The idea of receiving forgiveness from a priest against whom I had not sinned didn't make sense, nor could I agree that a pope could be less prone to error than anyone else. Perhaps the seed of a "priesthood of believers" concept was starting to grow in my spiritual understanding; certainly my sense of democratic individualism influenced my thinking.

I attended mass for two years and enjoyed the personal caring and feeling of acceptance I received from priests and laity alike. They knew I wasn't Catholic, but they welcomed me as a family friend. This sense of church community was profoundly attractive and explains why I stayed with Catholicism for as long as I did.

It also partially explains why I became a Mennonite. My theological quest, based on scant biblical knowledge, led me to be rebaptized at age twenty, but into no particular congregation or denomination. I had an idea that my commitment should be made public, but I still had no clear understanding of the church as Christ's body. Then I changed schools and cities, effectively though unintentionally severing my ties with the young Christians to whom I had been informally attached. Though I tried to maintain my faith commitment, the need to belong in my peer group was too strong. Ironically, though the school I now attended was church-affiliated, the prevailing attitude was secular. Besides the high incidence of drunkenness and violence among the students, the faculty showed almost no interest in active Christianity. The few who did were openly ridiculed by the students. To be accepted, I put my spiritual quest on hold.

So, after two years of Catholic mass, I spent two years in almost no church at all. True, there were chapel services on campus which I attended infrequently, but the students

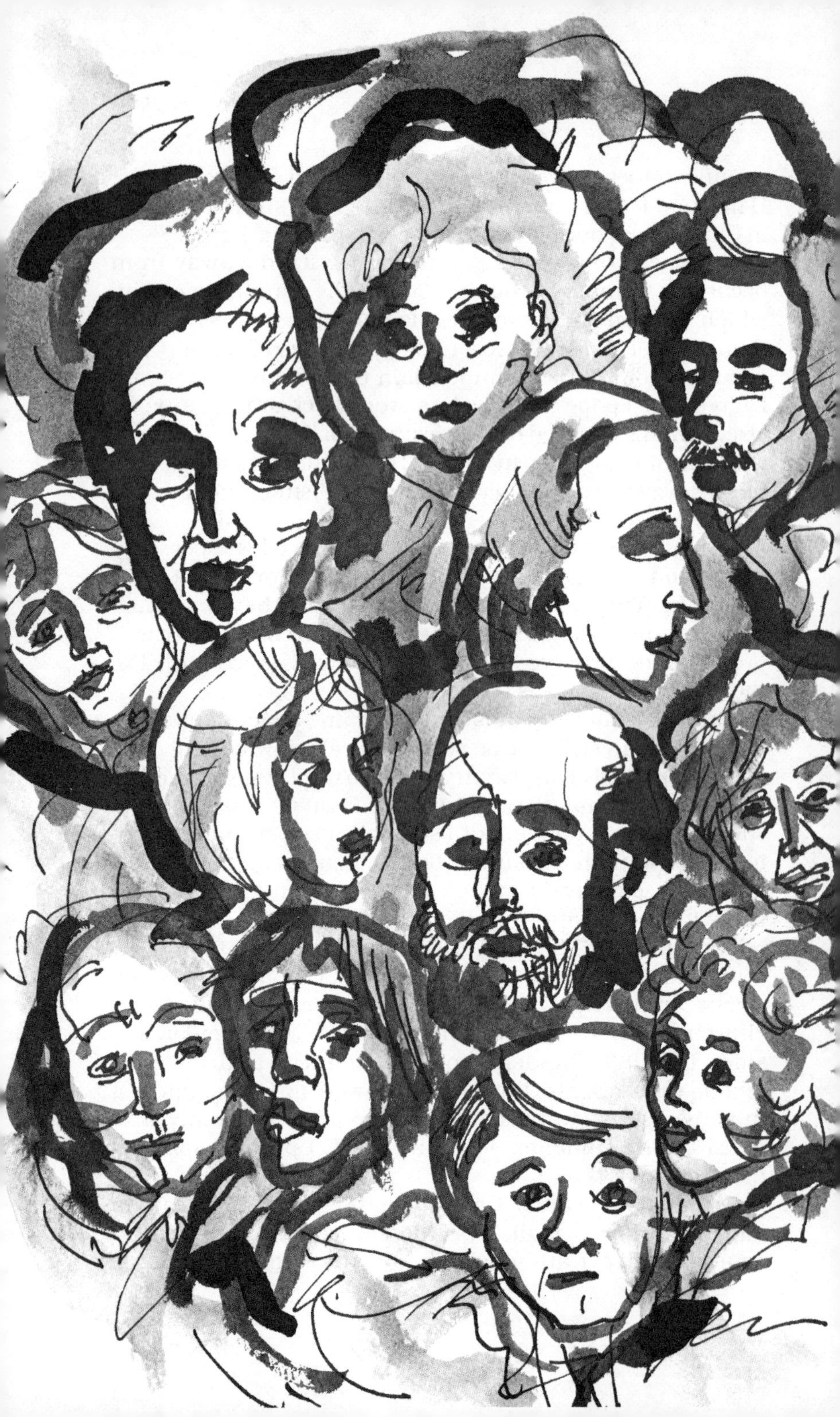

active in the chapel associations were mainly social outcasts. I wasn't self-confident enough to ignore such pressures, and besides, many of the issues with which I struggled were foreign to the chapel students. How does one have meaningful dialogue concerning sexuality with a person who has never been on a date? (At least the priests and nuns I knew had made informed decisions concerning celibacy.) Also, because of the direction my theology was taking, I found I didn't fit into any of the denominations around me.

A friend of a friend of my mother's put me on to Mennonites. This woman's granddaughter was serving in Mennonite Voluntary Service, teaching English to Mexican-Americans. I was ready to commit myself to similar service and phoned the granddaughter long-distance to find out more. What impressed me most was that she herself was not Mennonite yet praised the VS program and the church highly. The clincher came when she assured me that Mennonites would not try to force their beliefs on me. After I wrote to the Board of Missions for an official application, I gradually realized that my theology was Mennonite theology. I can't begin to describe the joy and relief I felt at this discovery. Finally I could wholeheartedly belong somewhere, with likeminded Christians who could help me apply my faith to my life. Since their beliefs were my beliefs, I would willingly submit to their gentle, even unwitting discipline in order to change some of the destructive habits I had acquired during my years of not belonging anywhere. It was a frightening but freely-made choice. After all, how different could Mennonites be if we shared the same convictions?

The first hints of the answer came to me at VS orientation. I was one of about twenty volunteers (VS'ers) ranging in age from eighteen to seventy-two, with the majority between twenty and twenty-five (I was twenty-two). The planned, week-long program was excellent, dealing with sensitive issues such as homosexuality, methods of social change, and maintaining one's Christian integrity while relating to people on their own levels. But the VS'ers seemed like people from a different planet. None of them had ever lived in a large city (except me), none of them had knowingly made friends with a homosexual (except me), and none of them knew what marijuana smelled like (except me). How could they possibly talk to the people in their VS communities? All of them knew what shoofly pie tasted like (except me), all of them knew the 606 doxology by heart (except me) and all of them knew cousins or sisters-in-law or neighbors of everyone else there (except me). We had very little to say to one another.

One incident, in particular, still upsets me. We were scheduled to see a play at an experimental theater in Chicago. One VS'er, age twenty-five, happened to see a list of the props while we were milling around in the tiny theater before curtain time. Because they included bedsheets and pillows, he decided the play wasn't fit for him to see, so he wandered off, rejoining the group after the performance. He was smug about this later. I still wonder how he coped in his assignment with delinquent boys.

The orientation coordinator, a black woman, empathized with me in my bewilderment and became my refuge. After being set loose in a slum area of Chicago in order to "relate" to the residents for three hours, I went into a shoe store, bought a five dollar pair of runners and struck up a conversation with the delighted salesman by asking him what was good and bad about the neighborhood because I was thinking of moving to that area. I probably learned more than the other VS'ers did, but their response to my story was to accuse me of lying to the salesman. The coordinator let me cry without judging me. In fact, she took me to her favorite restaurant—which was also a bar—after exacting a promise that I wouldn't tell the others of our destination. (Neither of us ordered drinks—I had signed a pledge renouncing personal alcohol consumption for the duration of my service assignment—but somehow the discovery of our presence in that place would have marked us as "not right.")

That week helped me to formulate an essential question which had long existed indistinctly in the background of my search for a church: What does it mean for me to be in the world, but not of it? Or, how do I "belong" and yet retain my personal identity? The question applies as well to the church. How can the church reach beyond itself without losing its characteristic separateness? Or, how can we truly become God's people?

Some observations:

(1) The strength of a tradition is also its weakness. In the close/closed community typical of certain religious perspectives such as Catholicism, Judaism, and Anabaptism, peoplehood is central to theological self-understanding. Further, it fulfills the very important psychological need of an individual to feel accepted and "owned." However, the flip side of this feature is its negative power to crush a person's feeling of self-worth. Conditional acceptance often rejects the newcomer's past experiences and individual member's uniqueness as being irrelevant or even sinful. Yet *without* standards there is the risk of collapsing into "no-peoplehood."

(2) Sometimes peripheral considerations crowd out essential ones. For example, many of the more conservative groups have bound their members to a strict community standard in which individual variations threaten the community's existence. Thus, groups split over whether to wear buttons or hooks or whether to drive on steel rims or rubber tires. For refugees from these groups, Protestant individualism becomes a welcome avenue of escape from a church community gone wrong. Yet, important as one's personal contact with God may be, it needs to be balanced with a healthy awareness of horizontal relationships, among church members and between the church body and the larger world.

Are Millers, Yoders, and Hershbergers automatically Mennonites? If so, in what sense? What links them to Sauders and Brubachers or Wiebes and Friesens? If 450 years of European history make us a people, where do Makanyangas and Chans fit? We must beware of cultural imperialism—insisting that converts adopt certain ethnic or social practices as signs of spiritual change.

I eventually tasted shoofly pie (I hated it), and learned hymn 606 by heart, and began to participate in the Mennonite Game. (I love it when people ask me who my father is, and all they can do when I tell them is smile vacantly but politely.) But is that when I became a Mennonite? During my first VS assignment I worked on an Indian reserve in Mississippi where elderly Choctaw women attended church in their traditional bead-ornamented dresses and Mennonite prayer coverings. They didn't understand much of what was preached, but somehow they got the idea that being Mennonite meant wearing a prayer covering. I pray they didn't come to understand Christianity that way.

My experience with various faith traditions has taught me that the church's most powerful drawing card is the offer of "home"—not some future pie-in-the-sky-when-you-die, but a circle of caring human beings who will help one work out how to live as a Christian. This sense of belonging is not created by rule books or behavioral codes; such devices have the effect of keeping people out rather than welcoming them in. Nor is home, in this sense, a place into which one is born. Our practice of adult baptism highlights the importance of choosing freely to participate in one's adopted family. Ideally, home is where I am loved no matter what, where I can come when no one else will have me. Home is where people know me well enough to spot my weaknesses and help me overcome them. Home is *not* a place to avoid until my behavior measures up to an impossible standard.

Without standards of delineation there is the risk of collapsing into "no-peoplehood." At stake, however, are not the standards themselves but the process by which they come about. Our Anabaptist ancestors worked out their identity around the communal concepts of consensus, the priesthood of believers, and the importance of each church member to the function of the whole. Though the issues and challenges of our situation continue to change, we can build on this tradition to become the caring community, strengthening and calling one another to be all we can be as persons and as God's people.

Lynne Martin is completing her master's degree in English at the University of Manitoba, Winnipeg.

QUESTIONS FOR REFLECTION AND DISCUSSION

Chapter 1. Living in the Nuclear Family

1. We define "family" according to a static, traditional social pattern that has virtually disappeared in our rapidly changing technologically oriented age. What are the elements of "family" based on past experience that we wish to preserve? What are the elements of "family" that need to be redefined or changed? What are some alternative "family" arrangements?

2. Many of the personal problems in the nuclear family originate in the socioeconomic structure surrounding it. Which employment factors contribute to the "family crisis"? Which of these factors need to be resisted or changed? What are some alternative economic arrangements?

3. Breaking inherited patterns and creating new ones is a difficult and often painful process. What are some of the problems arising from this struggle? What are some of the ways we can support each other in revitalizing the "family"?

Chapter 2. Being Single

1. Singleness has often been defined negatively because it is measured against a fixed norm, marriage. How can we describe singleness positively?

2. What are some of the benefits from allowing greater diversity in life choice, i.e., singleness, childlessness, single parenting? How can we support this process in each other?

3. Do you have friends who are single? What are they saying about the joys and problems of the single life?

Chapter 3. Being a Woman in a Man's World

1. The first step in fighting sexual discrimination is rec-

ognizing it. How have you experienced discrimination against women (a) in the social structures you participate in; (b) in other people's expectations; (c) in yourself?

2. What do you think are the main factors in the widespread imbalance of economic/political/social power in favor of men? What are some ways of fighting these?

3. How can we (women and men) support each other in creating equal opportunities for women in public and private life? What benefits do you see in the liberation of women: for women, men, children, and society as a whole?

Chapter 4. Working Mother

1. Mothers with young children have always worked, but only recently have they begun in significant numbers to work outside the home for pay. What factors have contributed to this major change?

2. Having and caring for children could be rewarded as a valuable contribution to society instead of penalized as a private indulgence. How would this change our concepts of (a) working for pay; (b) "work" and "family" as conflicting responsibilities; (c) maternity leave; (d) social advancement/achievement?

3. What are some alternative work/family arrangements? How can we support families with young children in their struggle to lead integrated lives?

Chapter 5. Learning to Live with Disabilities

1. Disabled persons have been identified negatively because they are measured against a fixed norm of "ability" and "achievement." How can they be identified positively? How does this change our understanding of "success" and accomplishment?

2. Do you agree with Harold Wilke that we tend to avoid handicapped people because of our own fears? What can we do about this?

3. How can we support each other in (a) coping with disabilities; (b) creating alternative social arrangements which recognize disabled persons as full and equal participants?

Questions for Reflection and Discussion

Chapter 6. Searching for Shalom in Mennonite Athletics

1. Do the factors Glick described contribute to aggression in athletics in your community? (How do sports get linked with militarism, sexism, and violence?)
2. Emphasizing "how one plays the game" rather than winning has implications beyond athletics. Compare with strategies in education, employment, and politics.
3. What are some noncompetitive alternatives in sports and other areas of social activity?

Chapter 7. Understanding Sexuality

1. Affirming our sexuality means living in tension with traditional attitudes of judgment and secrecy on the one hand, and contemporary attitudes of permissiveness and abuse on the other. How can we identify our sexuality positively?
2. Sex is often equated with genital intercourse and therefore with an exclusive marital relationship. If we acknowledge sexuality as an expression of our male- and female-ness (see also *Being Single*, p. 7), how does this change our perception of sexual behavior and the rules by which we evaluate it?
3. How can we be brothers and sisters to each other in the church with regard to this area of life? How do Schrag's comments on the need for touching and for nonsexual intimacy relate to this question?

Chapter 8. Parenting Parents

1. Illness and death come unplanned but we can anticipate them to some extent. How could we restructure "work" and "family" to take into account our mortality?
2. How can we support each other in the process of dying and looking after the dying?
3. The high incidence of cancer in our society is changing our experience of terminal illness and dying. What are some of the factors in this change? How can we respond positively to new demands and needs brought about by the occurrence and treatment of cancer?

Chapter 9. Life After Divorce

1. Divorce, as a failure in relationship, may be more pain-

ful than losing a partner through death. What external factors contribute to the anguish of separation and divorce? How can we support each other through crises of failure and new beginnings?

2. What social factors contribute to the rapid increase in divorce rates in our time? Which of these can be changed? How?

Chapter 10. Losing a Mate

1. There is a reasonable probability in our society that a wife will survive her husband. How does this expectation affect the way we plan and approach old age? What are the separate needs of men and women anticipating the event of widowhood?

2. For women who have spent most of their lives in an economically dependent, psychologically supportive role, widowhood represents a major identity crisis. What factors contribute to this crisis?

3. How can we support widows in their task of making new beginnings (often in old age)?

Chapter 11. Surviving Suicide

1. Which aspects of our religious and cultural heritage contribute to the destructive cycle of judgment/inadequacy/guilt as a response to personal crisis? How can we work together at creating a more sympathetic and supportive context for realizing our humanness?

2. "Living with unanswered questions" and "being at peace with uncertainty" describe faith as an open-ended, creative response of life's unpredictability, instead of a fixed belief in a prescribed formula. Are we comfortable with this approach? What implications does it have for other aspects of religious and social life?

Chapter 12. Homosexuality: Two Perspectives

1. Homosexuality is a "loaded" topic, hence, discussion needs to take into account the emotional predisposition of the participants. In your own response to homosexuality, which aspects are "prejudged" and which are a response to personal experience?

2. A difficult choice for homosexuals to make is between (a) silence, with its inherent dynamic of repression/denial/

Questions for Reflection and Discussion

schizophrenic identity; and (b) loss of friends, family relationships, social status, including very often jobs and job qualifications. How can we help make this choice less difficult?

3. What implications does a positive understanding of sexuality (see also *Understanding Sexuality*, p.51) have for the experience of homosexuals?

Chapter 13. Becoming God's People

1. Lynne Martin raises an important issue: the tension between maintaining standards and remaining open and accepting. How can the church reach beyond itself without losing its characteristic separateness?

2. How well does your church community do at integrating persons of other backgrounds and other church communions into the fellowship? How could you do better?

3. According to Martin, the church's most powerful drawing card is the offer of "home"—a circle of caring human beings who will help each other work out how to live as Christians. How do we create such a "home"? What does it mean to become brothers and sisters?